Peter Hunt's
Cape Cod Cookbook

By the same author

PETER HUNT'S
HOW-TO-DO-IT BOOK

PETER HUNT'S
WORKBOOK

Peter Hunt's
Cape Cod Cookbook

ILLUSTRATED BY THE AUTHOR

Gramercy Publishing Company, New York

This edition published by Gramercy Publishing Co., a division of Crown Publishers, Inc., by arrangement with the copyright owners

m n o p

Contents

Introduction

The practice of fine cooking on Cape Cod can easily be divided into three parts—New England, Portuguese and what might be called "Sophisticated." Cooking here can hardly be called local any more.

The original settlers, even from the days of the Mayflower, were practitioners of plain, good, substantial and nourishing dishes, prepared from what they produced on their own land, shot in the woods and fields near their homes and brought in from the sea around them. Very fine food indeed, and much of it unexcelled today.

As it is the world over, there are always some families who dine better than others. Their "touch," with the same ingredients that the people even next door use, is a little finer—they have imagination and an interest and a pride that makes their meals outstanding. Many Cape Cod brides sailed with their husbands in their own vessels to Europe and Asia, and their cooking was naturally influenced by what they tasted in foreign ports. In an early diary of one such bride, that Carl Dornbusch found in the house he bought in Wellfleet, the girl's interest in collecting recipes was important to her happiness, indeed. "I even wonder what the Egyptians ate and if their manners were exquisite," she writes the day after they left the Port of Leghorn.

I'm always amazed at what a lot of flour and milk and eggs and butter and dreary-looking materials can become in the hands of an interested cook.

The food that interests me perhaps the most on Cape Cod is that which the Portuguese prepare. Very few, if any, of the fishermen here are from the mainland; the great majority have come directly from the Azores, and their dishes are entirely regional and uninfluenced. I haven't any figures for the fact, but I am sure they have been permanently settled in Provincetown for at least four generations and it may be for a longer time than that. In most of the homes today the food is still prepared exactly as they prepared it in their homeland. Our town is now, of course, a famous tourist resort during the summer and I have long regretted that I haven't the ability, or the energy, to have an inn in which only Portuguese food is served. I can see it as if it were an actuality, complete to the last neat detail, and highly successful. It is an unassuming, weather-beaten place at the edge of the sea, as I picture it, with the sand dunes around it. There are piles of clam shells and oyster shells in the offing and, naturally, curious sea gulls are floating around the building.

It is all of pine and driftwood and white-washed walls inside and not too large, and extremely clean and neat and leisurely. There should be no fixed hours for meals in this inn. A bowl of cabbage soup flavored with mint when you come from swimming, fish or meat prepared in *vinha d'alhoes* when you are really hungry, or *couvres* or *linquiça* in Portuguese rolls. We could have *suspiros* or *trutas*, their wonderful Christmas cakes, every day of the year with a glass of deep red wine, or thick black coffee in thick white cups.

I think it would be a wonderful inn indeed, with driftwood burning on foggy and rainy days, and the smell of the sea about it always. I would be very happy in such a place and with such food.

The contrast to all this is, of course, the people whose circumstances make it possible for them to live on Cape Cod only during the summer months. Most of them love the Cape as dearly as I do and the majority of them bought old houses and restored them just about the time I came here. Their cooks and I have become great friends, too, through the years. I'm happy indeed that they are gracious enough to allow me to include in this book their dishes which I think most outstanding—the *spécialités de la maison*.

PETER HUNT

Peter Hunt's
Cape Cod Cookbook

The Portuguese
Are Wonderful Cooks

Portuguese Cooking

Maline Costa owns "The Moors"—an institution in our town and famous for Portuguese dishes. It is an informal place on the edge of the dunes on the road which leads to our great bathing beach.

People are always dropping in on their way back and forth for a bowl of kale soup or for *linquiça* or *vinha d'alhoes*—famous Portuguese dishes which are served only in his place.

At night there is music, guitar and piano, and singing—and a good bar; as it should be in all Latin places. But I am there usually in the daytime for the Portuguese dishes which Maline and Vivian have had cooked for me and which I am proud to start this book with before they are forgotten; there are so few places in America where one can order Portuguese food.

In case you are an "off-Caper" I should preface these recipes by explaining that *linquiça*, which will be mentioned often, is a highly spiced sausage which I find is used in much of their cooking. We can buy it now in most stores on Cape Cod. Mary Cordeiro's mother substitutes soup-meat for it at times when she wants a less pungent dish and the result is very satisfactory indeed.

COUVRES

(PORTUGUESE KALE SOUP)

1 pound pea beans
2 pounds kale
½ pound *linquiça*
6 small potatoes

Wash and boil the beans until tender. Add the remaining ingredients, cut in pieces. Cover with water. Cook 1 hour longer. Serves 6.

This is the simplest recipe for *couvres* and the one prepared in most of the fishermen's homes here. It is a very popular dish and a great stand-by.

The following is another version of the same soup which I like very much. Both dishes are hearty ones and are very filling. Often we have just a bowl of this soup for lunch—with bread and cheese. A cup of it is also wonderful any time on a cold day.

PORTUGUESE KALE SOUP

1 cup pea beans
1 large onion, sliced
1 pound *choriço* (highly spiced sausage)
1 pound kale
1 tablespoon salt
½ teaspoon pepper
1 tablespoon vinegar
2 cups cubed potatoes

Soak beans overnight in cold water. In the morning, drain, add the onion, sausage (cut in pieces), kale (broken in pieces), salt and pepper and vinegar, and 10 cups water. Bring to boil, reduce heat and cook gently 2 to 3 hours. Add potatoes and 1 additional cup water. Continue cooking until potatoes are tender. Serves 6.

CABBAGE SOUP

½ cup yellow-eye beans
1 small onion, chopped
1 small cabbage
4 medium potatoes
½ pound *linquiça*
salt and pepper to taste

Soak beans overnight. Drain and place in kettle. Add onion. Cover beans with water and boil until cooked. Add cabbage, potatoes, *linquiça* cut in 1-inch slices, salt and pepper. Cook until cabbage and potatoes are well done. The flavor of this soup is even better when reheated the next day. Serves 6.

When I first tried this recipe I thought that one onion didn't sound as if it would be efficient—so I used two. The subtlety of one onion is amazing, however. So never use two.

Here again are two versions of Portuguese Fish Chowder. Both are equally delicious—according to one's taste.

PORTUGUESE FISH CHOWDER

½ cup salt pork cubes
1 cup chopped onion
3 cups diced potatoes
1 teaspoon salt
¼ teaspoon pepper
½ teaspoon saffron
1 tablespoon vinegar
2 pounds lean fish (haddock, whiting or flounder)
    cut in chunks

In deep, heavy kettle, try out pork cubes slowly, turning occasionally, until only crisp pork bits remain. Remove these to use later. In the hot fat, fry onion slowly until soft and golden. Add 6 cups cold water, potatoes, seasonings and vinegar. Boil until potatoes are half done. Add fish. Continue cooking gently until fish is tender. Add browned bits of pork. Serves 6.

PORTUGUESE FISH CHOWDER

1 small codfish or haddock, cut in chunks
1 onion, sliced
2 tablespoons vinegar
4 potatoes
¼ teaspoon ground cumin seed
½ teaspoon saffron
salt and pepper

Place fish and onion in a kettle and cover with water. Add vinegar immediately. When fish is cooked, add remaining ingredients. Serves 6.

PORTUGUESE STYLE
FISH CHOWDER

1 tablespoon shortening
2 good-sized onions
1 No. 2 can tomatoes
1 teaspoon salt
1 good-sized pepper
6 potatoes
4 pounds fish (haddock or cod)
1 tablespoon vinegar
pinch of saffron

Add onions to shortening and brown them slightly. Add tomatoes, salt and hot pepper. Cut up potatoes and add to above with 8 cups water. Cook for 20 minutes. Add fish cut in pieces, vinegar and saffron at same time. Cook for 10 minutes more. Serve piping hot. Serves 6.

FRIED FISH
WITH MOLHO CRU
(MOLHO CRU IS A POPULAR SAUCE IN THE AZORES SERVED ALWAYS ON COLD FRIED FISH)

2 pounds fish (cod, haddock or flounder)
seasoned flour for coating
1 cup vinegar
1 bay leaf
¼ teaspoon saffron
½ cup minced onion

Roll fish in flour seasoned with salt and pepper. Fry in heated fat, turning to brown nicely on both sides. Chill fish.
Make sauce by combining vinegar, bay leaf, saffron and onion. Pour over fish on platter.

VINHA D'ALHOES
(FOR MARINATING FISH AND MEATS)

1 cup vinegar
3 cups water
2 minced garlic cloves
pinch of cumin seed
1 teaspoon salt
½ teaspoon black pepper

In the above pickling combination we, in our house, soak overnight either codfish, haddock or flounder cut into pieces suitable in size for serving. Just before cooking, remove the fish from the liquid, dry well, dip in meal and fry.

Mary Souza, who has managed our kitchen these last five years, has shown us that pork chops "galvanized" (what an expression!) this same way are equally delicious. It is one of the favorite dishes in our house now.

CLAM BOIL

In a big covered kettle place these ingredients in layers in the order given:

Clams (steamers)
Onions (whole, but peeled)
Pork sausages (wrapped in wax paper)
Potatoes in jackets
Eggs in shell

and, individually wrapped in wax paper:

Corn on the cob
Linquiça (Portuguese sausage)
Frankfurters or Tripe

Cook for 1½ hours. This is wonderful for a summer evening's picnic. A cup of water in the bottom of the kettle is sufficient to start the steam: the opening clams quickly add their liquid.

This is the one recipe I know where you must use your own judgment as to the quantity of each ingredient according to the number of people served and according to their appetites.

I know only mine:
- 12 clams
- 1 onion
- 1 pork sausage
- 1 potato
- 1 egg
- 2 ears of corn

And by that time I'm appreciative just for the flavor of the *linquiça*, frankfurters and/or tripe which has gloriously permeated everything else. It is wise indeed to know your guests' appetites when preparing this wonderful picnic. Serve beer with it, and black coffee just as you are starting home.

PORTUGUESE SQUID STEW

- 3 pounds squid
- 3 large onions, chopped
- 1 No. 2 can tomatoes
- 2 tablespoons fat or oil
- 1 tablespoon red pepper
- 5 large potatoes, cubed
- 1 tablespoon salt
- 1 tablespoon vinegar

Clean and wash squid and cut in 2-inch slices. Fry onions in fat or oil until light brown. Add tomatoes and red pepper. Stew squid in this mixture for 2 hours over a low flame. Add potatoes and salt. When potatoes are done, add vinegar. Serves 6 to 8.

A wonderful dish that should be better known.

STEAMED HADDOCK

(WITH SWEET SOUR SAUCE)

1½ pounds haddock
1 onion
1 bay leaf
1 sprig parsley
½ teaspoon salt
⅛ teaspoon pepper
3 carrots
2 tablespoons butter
1 tablespoon flour
2 tablespoons vinegar
1 teaspoon chopped parsley

Place fish on trivet in pressure cooker. Add 1 cup water, onion, bay leaf, parsley sprig, salt, pepper and carrots. Cover and cook under 10 pounds pressure for 5 minutes. Reduce pressure by cooling pressure cooker under running water. Place fish on hot platter. Force onion and carrots through a coarse sieve. Add to strained broth in cooker. Brown the butter in another pan, add flour. Gradually add broth and stir until blended. Add vinegar, chopped parsley and a little salt. Pour over fish. Serves 4.

FRIED SALTED
CODFISH SCRAPPLE

1 cup yellow corn meal
2 cups shredded codfish
1 small onion
¼ teaspoon pepper
¼ teaspoon dry mustard
½ teaspoon poultry seasoning
1½ teaspoons salt
⅔ cup flour
fat for frying

Mix corn meal with 1 cup of cold water. Slowly add to 3 cups boiling water. Cook 10 minutes, stirring often. Soak salted codfish until soft enough to shred easily. Remove from water and shred. Add the shredded codfish, onion and seasonings to the corn meal mixture. Pour into oiled loaf pan, chill. Cut into ½-inch slices. Dip each slice in flour and brown on sides in a little fat on a griddle. Serves 6.

MOLHO COSIDO
(PORTUGUESE SAUCE FOR FISH)

2 large onions
1 tablespoon flour
½ teaspoon ground saffron
¼ teaspoon ground allspice
2 tablespoons vinegar
1 small can tomatoes (optional)

Slice onions and fry in a little bacon fat until clear. Add flour and stir. Add 1½ cups water, spices and vinegar and cook until thick.

Good on cold fried fish or roast meat.

BACALHAU A PORTUGUESA

(SALT COD A LA PORTUGUESE)

1½ pounds dry salt cod
4 large potatoes
5 onions
5 tomatoes
5 pimientos
2 tablespoons oil
2 tablespoons melted butter
salt and pepper

Soak cod overnight in cold water. Drain. Remove bones and flake the fish. Slice potatoes, onions, tomatoes and pimientos, and place in alternate layers with fish in deep earthenware casserole. Add melted butter and oil. Season with salt and pepper. Simmer for 1½ hours, keeping the casserole covered. Serves 6.

STEWED HAKE

2 small hake
2 large onions, sliced
1 tablespoon fat
1 tablespoon flour
1 tablespoon vinegar
¼ teaspoon each: ground cloves, allspice,
        black pepper, cinnamon
½ teaspoon saffron
½ teaspoon ground cumin seed
1 teaspoon salt

Clean, wash and cut up hake. Fry the onion in the fat until slightly brown. Add flour and mix thoroughly, until brown. Add 2 cups water, vinegar and spices. Place fish in this gravy and cook for 15 minutes. When tested, the fish will leave the bone. Serves 6.

RABBIT FRICASSEE, PORTUGUESE STYLE

1 domestic rabbit
1½ teaspoons salt
¼ teaspoon pepper
½ teaspoon saffron
1 large onion, chopped fine
1 tablespoon vinegar
fat for frying

Cut rabbit in serving-size pieces. Cover and allow to stand in cool place several hours or overnight. Mix together salt, pepper, saffron, and rub into meat. Heat fat in deep, heavy skillet, to depth of 1 inch. Fry rabbit slowly until brown on all sides. Place onion in bottom of a casserole; arrange rabbit on top of onion. Combine vinegar and ½ cup water; pour over rabbit. Cover tightly; bake in slow oven (275°) for 2 hours. Serves 6.

FRANKFURTER STEW

1 tablespoon shortening
2 medium onions
1 pound frankfurters
3 boiled potatoes, cold, diced
⅛ teaspoon salt
⅛ teaspoon pepper
dash of Tabasco sauce
1 tablespoon vinegar

Fry onions in the shortening until golden brown. Add frankfurters and fry lightly. Add 1 cup cold water, salt, pepper and tabasco sauce. Simmer for ½ hour, then add potatoes. Take from fire. Add vinegar. Serves 6 to 8.

GRAO DE BICO
(CHICK PEAS, PORTUGUESE STYLE)

½ pound chick peas
¼ pound *linquiça*
1 medium onion, chopped
1½ teaspoons salt
1 tablespoon vinegar

Wash peas. Soak overnight in enough cold water to cover. Drain peas and place in kettle. Cover with fresh cold water. Add sausage, cut in pieces, onion, salt and vinegar. Bring to boil. Reduce heat to low and cook 3 hours. Serves 6.

PORTUGUESE EASTER BREAD

Winter is never severe on Cape Cod but it is apt to seem long and grey during March. But I often wonder if March isn't a month that should be spent in traveling—winter isn't over, spring hasn't come. It's exciting then to come back here in the beginning of April and watch the breeze quicken the lakes and see the buds starting on the willows and know that the crocuses and the tulips will soon be in bloom. And the frogs will be heard any day in the marshes—that's a nice sound, indeed.

And we're always happy—after a spell of doldrums. So it's a pleasant custom to give a present to a friend to show your happiness. The Portuguese here have the fine custom of bringing their friends a loaf of bread, an especial bread which they make only once a year, and which we are always honored to receive.

PORTUGUESE EASTER BREAD

3 yeast cakes
12 cups flour
1 tablespoon salt
3 cups sugar
12 eggs, well beaten
1 pint lukewarm milk
½ pound butter, melted

Dissolve yeast cakes in 1 cup lukewarm water and set aside. Sift flour and salt together, in a large pan. Mix the sugar and well-beaten eggs with the lukewarm milk. Add this mixture to the flour. Add yeast. Knead all this until it has the consistency of bread dough. Lastly, add the melted shortening, kneading a little more, and adding more milk, if necessary. Cover and let rise until double in bulk (usually overnight). Divide the dough into round, slightly flat loaves, roll in flour, place in greased pie plates.

On top of each loaf, if desired, press into dough a raw egg (still in shell which has been washed in cold water). Place 1 or 2 strips of dough over egg and let rise again. For a glaze, pat milk over loaf before placing in oven. Bake slowly in moderate oven (350°) until golden brown. Should make 12 to 15 loaves.

As with every other race, there is much visiting among Portuguese friends at Christmas time. The "Menino Jesus"—a terraced crèche arranged with flowers and lighted candles and treasured carvings from the Islands is now the center of display. We go from house to house admiring the beautiful decorations and offering our felicitations each year. *Suspiros* and *trutas* are traditionally served with wine.

SUSPIROS

(SIGHS)

3 egg whites
1 cup sugar
½ teaspoon lemon juice
½ cup almond meats

Beat egg whites until *very* stiff. Add sugar gradually. Add lemon juice. *Roll* in almond meats. Line a cookie sheet with brown paper. Drop mixture by teaspoonfuls onto this paper and place in moderate (350°) oven. Remove when slightly brown. Should make 1 dozen.

Almonds should be prepared ahead of time. Blanch almonds in boiling water. Remove skins and cut lengthwise into thin strips. (Shredded coconut may be substituted, but almonds make these far superior.)

TRUTAS

(A PASTRY FILLED WITH SWEET POTATO)

Filling:
1 pound sweet potatoes
1½ cups sugar
grated rind of ¼ lemon
½ teaspoon cinnamon

Boil potatoes in skins. Peel and mash. Add sugar, lemon rind and cinnamon. Cook for 1 minute, stirring constantly. Set aside to cool.

Dough:
5 cups all-purpose flour
1 teaspoon salt
juice of 4 oranges
½ pound butter
⅔ cup shortening
1 wineglass brandy

Have butter and shortening at room temperature. Proceed as for pie crust, using brandy (or whiskey) and orange juice instead of water. Roll out very thin and cut as for turnovers, using a pastry cutter to help seal crust. Place filling in (cookie-size) turnover before sealing. Fry in deep fat until golden brown. Drain on brown paper. When cold, roll in powdered sugar. Makes 3 dozen.

PORTUGUESE POT ROAST

5 pounds beef
salt and pepper to taste
1 medium can (pint size) tomatoes
1 pound onions
5 medium potatoes (whole)
1 bunch carrots
1 good-sized turnip
1 tablespoon vinegar

Wash meat, place in pan and sear on all sides until brown. Sprinkle with salt and pepper. Pour tomatoes over the meat. Cut onions in rings over meat. Add water enough to cover meat and let simmer slowly for 3 hours. When meat is ¾ cooked, add potatoes, carrots, turnip and vinegar. Keep adding water, if necessary, until cooked. Serves 6 to 8.

RED KIDNEY BEAN SOUP

small piece salt pork
1 medium-sized onion
½ pound linquiça
1 large can (quart size) kidney beans
1 pound squash
1 pound sweet potatoes
2 white potatoes
salt and pepper

Cut pork in small pieces and try out. Add onion cut up small. Add linquica in 1-inch pieces. Cook for 4 minutes. Cut up squash and potatoes. Add, with the beans, to the above, cover with water and cook for 40 minutes over a low flame. Add salt and pepper to taste. Serves 6.

THESE RECIPES ARE

Tradition on Cape Cod...

AS TRADITIONAL AS THE PILGRIMS,
BAYBERRIES AND NOR'WEST STORMS

Oysters, Clams, Mussels and Scallops

When I first came to Provincetown, Colin Campbell Clements lived here and seemed to feel that he had discovered steamed clams. I, too, had never had the opportunity to dig clams until then, and hardly a day passed that summer that Clem didn't enthuse whoever he could find to go clamming with him.

We would always have a bucket of them on our porches being kept fresh in sea water, to which we had added a few tablespoons of cornmeal to purge the clams. Clams were our great discovery that year and whenever we were hungry we would scoop them out of the pail and steam them and eat them at all hours.

Steaming clams is perhaps the easiest kind of cooking I know. A cup of water to a pail of clams is sufficient to start the steam which will open the clams, but not enough to dilute and make weak the taste of the clam juice. Since then we have learnt to add a half clove of garlic to the water. This gives, of course, a subtle flavor and seems to bring out the taste of the sea, which I like very much.

Perhaps I never was more disappointed than one night in a famous inn in Chicago. It was a bitter cold night, cold as only Chicago can be, and a group of us from Cape Cod were delighted to see steamed clams on the menu. You can imagine our disgust and disappointment when six large sea clams, of all things, were served to us on a silver tray, *sous cloche*, and wrapped in a linen napkin.

No one can eat enough steamed clams. In our house a large bowl of them is placed in the middle of the table from which everybody helps himself, and always the bowl is replenished again and again each time we have them. No meal is more delicious than steamed clams dipped in drawn butter, together with cups of clam broth and Portuguese bread.

I have no idea if this, with watermelon, makes a balanced meal or not, but it is a wonderful meal for any summer's day under the old willow tree in our garden. We are fortunate enough to have collected years ago heavy white iron-stone plates and mugs and bowls which we always use when we serve steamed clams.

"Cherry stones" and "littlenecks" are quahaugs. They have hard shells and are delicious when eaten raw without "cocktail-sauce." I don't like "cocktail-sauce," a mixture of catsup, horse-radish and lemon juice. It deadens the taste of the clams, so I'm not including it in this book.

But quahaugs can be cooked in an infinite number of ways:

FRIED CLAMS

Dry, roll in flour, dip in beaten egg and roll in fine, dry crumbs. Fry in deep, hot fat until they are golden brown.

Drain on brown paper and serve with quartered lemon—or, if your taste is for catsup, with catsup. Most people I know consider 1 dozen fried clams their appetite.

CLAM FRITTERS

1 cup sifted flour
1 teaspoon baking powder
1 quart finely-chopped clams
1 beaten egg

Mix flour and baking powder together. Add the clams and the egg. Drop tablespoonfuls into hot fat in a deep skillet and fry until brown. Serves 6.

CLAM CHOWDER

1 quart soft-shell clams, ground in meat chopper
3 ounces salt pork, diced
1 onion, sliced
4 potatoes, sliced
1 pint milk
salt and pepper
butter

Try out the pork. Add the onion and fry until golden brown. Add the potatoes and the juice from the clams; cover with boiling water and let simmer until the potatoes are done. Add the clams and cook for 10 minutes. Just before serving add the milk, heated, seasoning and a good-sized lump of butter. Serves 6.

My father could never cook anything except clam chowder. He always made it in our house and he won a little fame for it. His secret, I believe, was the addition of a few bay leaves, which I wonder if other people use in their chowder.

MUSSELS

I don't know where else in this book to write about mussels. They are steamed as clams are steamed and are very delicious indeed.

Often Tiny Worthington and I and her dog and her cat—who follows us as the dog does—go down to the beach in North Truro and scrape deep purple mussels from the pilings of the old bridge there.

I always have great nostalgia for a small town called Hyères in the South of France when I eat mussels. It was there I had them the first time and it was perhaps one of the memorable meals of my life.

The armistice had just been signed and an elderly couple who were refugees from the north had been wonderful to a group of us in this hospital town. We had given them chocolate and tobacco—which was no deprivation to us at all as they were issued daily and in quantities greater than we could use. And for a few sous a day the wife did sewing for us, making costumes—scenery for amateur plays we improvised to while away the time of our recuperation. We learned that she once had been a circus performer, so by degrees she joined in and made, in a way, our little acts somewhat professional. A camaraderie, a bond greater than any of us realized, gradually asserted itself—and she was heartbroken when we were to be evacuated. Apparently our little existence and our small occupations had filled her depletion out of all proportion.

But a gesture must be made—to make our departure gay she gave us a farewell luncheon party.

It was a beautiful luncheon, one of the finest I ever have had. Mussels, which the old couple scraped from the rocks in the sea a few miles away, artichokes from a neighbor's garden. The kirsch poured on the sliced pineapple cost one franc in the cafe next door. A wonderful meal under a mimosa tree—and probably the last franc they would see in Heaven knows when.

CLAM OMELET

1 cup clams
1 heaping tablespoon butter
1 teaspoon salt
paprika
6 eggs, separated
⅔ cup cream

Wash clams, put through food chopper and sauté in melted butter. Add salt and paprika to egg yolks, beat until light. Add cream and chopped clams; mix thoroughly. Fold in stiffly-beaten egg whites. Pour mixture into a well-buttered omelet pan or skillet and bake in a moderate oven (350°) about 25 minutes, until brown. Serves 4 to 6.

CREAM OF QUAHAUG SOUP

24 quahaugs
½ cup liquid from quahaugs
2 sliced onions
3 cups milk
sprig parsley, minced
2 tablespoons butter
2 tablespoons flour
1 cup heavy cream
salt and pepper

Mince quahaugs. Add liquid and onions. Cook 5 minutes. Add milk, parsley and seasoning. Pour into a double boiler. Let stand, do not cook. Meanwhile, blend butter and flour. Stir into the soup. Cook 3 minutes. Strain. Add the cream. Serves 6.

CLAM PIE

2 cups sea clams, chopped fine
¼ cup clam liquor
1 tablespoon butter, melted
1 onion, cut up (optional)
pie crust
½ cup cracker crumbs
1 egg, well beaten
1 cup milk
salt and pepper

Melt butter in skillet, add clams, and other ingredients. Let simmer for 15 minutes. Place in deep pie plate, cover with pie crust. Bake until crust is golden brown. Serves 4.

OYSTER STEW

1 quart oysters
2 cups oyster liquor
2 cups milk
4 tablespoons butter
salt and pepper

Strain oyster liquor. Thoroughly wash oysters and add to liquor. Place on fire and cook for 5 minutes. Add milk and heat thoroughly, but do not allow to boil. Add butter, salt and pepper. Decorate each plate with a dash of red cayenne pepper. Serves 4.

Helene Biddle adds ¼ cup chopped celery stalks.

Inez Horton flavors hers with 1 teaspoon Worcestershire sauce.

A pinch of dried parsley pleases some people.

An especially delicious stew is made in exactly the same way, substituting chopped bay scallops for the oysters. With the scallops the celery is a necessity.

PICKLED OYSTERS

1 gallon oysters
2 tablespoons thyme leaves
2 tablespoons crushed bay leaves
2 tablespoons grated onion
1 tablespoon crushed parsley
1 tablespoon crushed fennel
1 tablespoon ground cloves
2 cloves garlic crushed to a pulp
2 teaspoons ground allspice
1 teaspoon crushed peppercorns
½ cup dry white wine to each quart jar

Strain the liquor from freshly opened oysters and scald it over a very low flame. Poach the oysters, a few at a time, in this liquor. Remove oysters and place them in an earthenware or glass container and set them aside. Add the herbs and spices to the oyster liquor. Boil up the oyster-herb liquor twice, remove it from the fire and let it cool. When the oysters and the spiced liquor are cold, pack the oysters in quart glass jars, and pour the pickle liquor over them, leaving enough space in each jar to add ½ cup dry white wine. Seal the jars and let them stand in a dark, cool place for at least 2 weeks before using. Be sure that your jars are sterilized before using.

OYSTERS
BAKED IN SHELLS

24 large oysters and shells
1 egg
1 cup bread crumbs
butter

Scrub shells carefully to remove sand. Beat egg with 1 tablespoon water. Dip cleaned oysters into egg mixture, roll in crumbs. Place oysters in shells, dot them with butter and bake in a quick oven (450°) 10 minutes. (I would suggest serving 6 oysters to each person.)

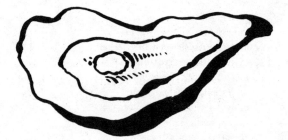

ESCALLOPED OYSTERS

1 pint oysters
½ teaspoon salt
¼ teaspoon paprika
1 tablespoon minced parsley
¼ cup minced celery
2 tablespoons butter
½ cup top cream
¼ cup dry crumbs mixed with 2 tablespoons melted butter

Butter a shallow baking dish and put in a thin layer of crumbs. Add a layer of oysters. Sprinkle with a little of the seasonings, parsley and celery. Dot oysters with bits of butter.

Repeat this procedure until dish is full, making the last layer of oysters. Pour over this the top cream. Cover with the buttered crumbs. Bake 30 minutes in moderate oven (350°). Serves 4 to 6.

ESCALLOPED SCALLOPS

1 pound scallops
1 cup soft bread crumbs
2 cups cracker crumbs
¾ cup melted butter
½ teaspoon salt
few grains pepper
1 cup light cream

Wash scallops in cold water; drain. Cut scallops in half crosswise. Combine crumbs, butter, salt and pepper. Alternate layers of scallops and crumb mixture in greased baking dish, ending with crumbs. Pour cream into baking dish. Bake in a moderate oven (350°) for 25 minutes. Serves 4 to 6.

ESCALLOPED OYSTERS AND SCALLOPS

1 quart oysters
1 pint scallops
1 cup cream
1 cup bread crumbs
½ cup melted butter
1 tablespoon celery seed
salt and pepper

Mix melted butter and bread crumbs together. Put a thin layer of this mixture in bottom of buttered baking dish. Cover with a layer of oysters and sprinkle with seasonings. Add some of the cream. Add a layer of scallops, seasonings. Add a layer of crumbs. Add another layer of oysters and balance of cream. Top with balance of scallops and buttered crumbs. Bake in hot oven (400°) for 30 minutes. Serves 6 to 8.

BAKED OYSTERS

½ cup dry bread crumbs
1 cup cracker crumbs
½ cup melted butter
2 dozen oysters
¼ teaspoon salt
⅛ teaspoon pepper
2 tablespoons oyster liquor
2 tablespoons milk

Mix bread and cracker crumbs. Add melted butter to crumbs. Line bottom of buttered shallow baking dish with ⅓ of this mixture. Cover with ½ of the oysters. Sprinkle with salt and pepper. Add 1 tablespoon each of oyster liquor and milk. Repeat this procedure. Top with crumbs. Bake in hot oven (400°) for 30 minutes. Serves 4 to 6.

LOBSTERS

Real Cape Codders are interested in lobster only two ways—boiled or broiled.

Boiled:
Personally, I think a boiled lobster retains the subtle taste of the sea best. And it's no chore at all to drop the lobster into a pan in which there is an inch or two of boiling water. Cover, and let it boil rapidly until it turns a brilliant red all over. Usually 15 to 20 minutes is enough but, of course, it all depends on the size of the lobster.

I prefer them about 1½ pounds. They are more succulent and tender this size. Split down the middle, crack the large claws and serve with drawn butter.

Broiled:
Split alive and remove the "craw sac" that is just in back of the head and the dark intestinal canal that runs through the body. Pack with bread crumbs and lumps of butter, and broil—preferably over charcoal—for about 20 minutes. Decorate with parsley and serve with drawn butter and quartered lemons.

These are the two ways most Cape Codders prepare lobster, but Colonel Richard Magee of Truro is famous for his lobster Cantonese:

LOBSTER CANTONESE

2 tablespoons oil
1 teaspoon salt
dash of pepper
1 crushed clove garlic
½ pound pork meat, chopped
1 teaspoon minced scallion
2 live baby lobsters
1 cup chicken bouillon
1 egg, slightly beaten
2 tablespoons cornstarch
1 tablespoon soy sauce

Cook oil, salt and pepper and garlic for 2 or 3 minutes. Remove garlic. Mix oil with chopped pork meat and minced scallion. Boil live lobsters just about 5 minutes. Cut each lobster in two lengthwise, leaving shells on, then across in 2-inch pieces. Cut claws in 3 sections. Cook lobster (in shells) and pork mixture in a covered pan for 10 minutes over a moderate flame, after you have added the chicken bouillon. Then add the egg, slightly beaten, and cook for 2 minutes, stirring constantly, without allowing it to boil. Blend ¼ cup water, cornstarch and soy sauce, add to the mixture and cook together for a few minutes until the sauce thickens. Serve with hot boiled rice. Serves 4 to 6.

LOBSTER SALAD

Lobster Salad is an easy dish to prepare and, for all its ease, is often a fine party dish—according to the way it is served.

Remove the meat from boiled lobsters—heavy lobsters, too large for boiling or broiling (because the meat is apt to be a bit stringy) are good here—and cut into pieces, not too small. Add a small amount, to suit your taste, of chopped tender white celery stalks. Arrange on crisp lettuce leaves, garnish with lobster claws, sliced hard-boiled eggs and capers. Chill well and serve with home-made mayonnaise.

MAYONNAISE

½ teaspoon dry mustard
1 teaspoon salt
2 teaspoons sugar
⅛ teaspoon pepper
2 egg yolks or 1 whole egg
1½ cups olive oil
2 tablespoons vinegar

Mix dry ingredients, add egg and beat slightly. Add oil a few drops at a time and beat vigorously after each addition until the mixture is thoroughly blended. As the dressing begins to thicken the oil may be added more rapidly. When it becomes quite stiff, thin with a little of the vinegar or lemon juice; then continue adding oil and vinegar or lemon juice alternately until all have been used. Egg yolks make a stiffer dressing than the whole egg.

Jessica and Manfred Perry always keep in their deep-freeze loaves of bread that have been scooped out and filled with lobster salad—or chicken salad. They always are prepared for a party.

Mabel Leaton serves lobster salad in a halved avocado.

LOBSTER NEWBURG

⅓ cup dry sherry
2 cups cooked lobster meat, coarsely cut
6 tablespoons butter
2 tablespoons flour
2½ cups milk
4 egg yolks, slightly beaten
¼ teaspoon salt
dash of nutmeg
dash of cayenne
toast points

Pour sherry over lobster in shallow dish; cover, let stand at least 30 minutes. Melt butter in top of double boiler directly over medium heat, stir in flour; cook until bubbly. Remove from heat; gradually stir in milk; cook over low heat until mixture comes to a boil and thickens, stirring constantly. Place over hot, not boiling, water. Stir a few tablespoons of the hot mixture into the egg yolks; blend well and slowly pour back into the hot mixture, stirring constantly. Cook and stir until thick, 3 to 5 minutes. Season to taste with salt, nutmeg, cayenne. Blend in the lobster and unabsorbed sherry. When heated serve on toast points. Serves 4.

BAKED FISH

(BASS, BLUEFISH, COD OR HADDOCK)

Baking a fish is a very simple procedure, but what a controversy it has caused in our neighborhood. "I use egg in my dressing—why don't you?" "Thyme?!! Sage is much better." "I don't understand how they made it so dry."

So I checked with most of the neighbors and all the procedures seem relatively the same. The seasonings in the dressing vary so slightly that I wonder about all the arguments and back-biting.

This is the method in our kitchen: Stuff a good-sized fish with either of the following dressings, sew the opening with needle and thread. Cut 3 or 4 gashes through the skin on each side. This keeps the fish in shape during the cooking. Lay 6 good-sized strips of salt pork over the top. Bake in very hot oven (550°) for the first 15 minutes, then reduce the heat to 425° and continue baking for 30 to 45 minutes according to the size of the fish. Allow ¾ to 1 pound of fish per person.

Surf-casting on the "back-shore"

NEW ENGLAND STUFFING

3 cups bread crumbs
2 small onions, chopped fine
sprinkle of thyme
1 beaten egg
½ teaspoon salt
⅛ teaspoon pepper

Mix well and moisten with water.

Oyster stuffing is wonderful with codfish:

OYSTER STUFFING

2 cups cracker crumbs
¼ cup melted butter
¼ teaspoon salt
1½ teaspoons lemon juice
⅛ teaspoon pepper
¼ teaspoon poultry seasoning
1½ tablespoons chopped onion
2 cups washed oysters
1½ tablespoons parsley, chopped fine

Mix ingredients lightly with fork.

TARTARE SAUCE

½ cup mayonnaise
½ tablespoon capers
½ tablespoon chopped pickle
½ teaspoon chopped olives
½ teaspoon chopped parsley

Mix all ingredients together.

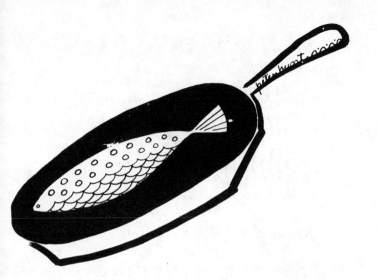

FILLET OF SOLE

Cut sole into long fillets. Sprinkle with salt and pepper. Roll fillets in flour. Dip them in beaten egg and roll in fine dry crumbs. Fry in deep fat at 350° until delicately browned. Serve with tartare sauce (p. 52). Plan on 1 or 2 fillets for each person, according to how well you know their appetites.

BOSTON BAKED BEANS

Beans and Brown Bread are as traditional in New England for Saturday night supper as the proverbial gag about the "Saturday night bath." I often wonder why I didn't care for them especially until I came to live here. Maybe because it was only an occasional dish where I came from.

Like many of the most usual dishes here, there is never an agreement among the different families as to how beans should be baked—with an onion or without, some like more molasses, some less. It's always that way, I suppose, among families in small towns, thank heavens.

BOSTON BAKED BEANS

3 cups pea beans
2 teaspoons salt
3 tablespoons molasses
2 tablespoons sugar
¼ teaspoon mustard
½ pound salt pork

Soak beans overnight in cold water. Then bring to simmering point and cook until skins begin to burst. Drain. Put in a bean pot. Add seasonings mixed with 1 cup boiling water.

Blanch the salt pork, scrape the surface of the rind and cut through every ½ inch. Bury it in the beans so that just the rind is exposed. Cover with boiling water and bake in a slow oven, adding more water from time to time. Bury a small onion in the beans for extra flavor. Bake 6 to 8 hours (300°). Serves 6.

BOSTON BROWN BREAD

1 cup rye meal
1 cup corn meal
1 cup coarse whole wheat flour
¾ tablespoon soda
1 teaspoon salt
¾ cup molasses
2 cups sour milk
1 cup seedless raisins

Mix and sift dry ingredients. Add molasses, milk and raisins, stir until well mixed, and fill well-greased mold ⅔ full. Cover tightly and place mold on rack in kettle containing boiling water, allowing water to come halfway up around mold. Cover kettle tightly and steam 3½ hours, keeping water at boiling point. Add more boiling water as needed. Take from water, remove cover, and set in slow oven (300°) 15 minutes to dry off. Remove from mold. Should serve 6 people but I suggest you make 2 loaves of this bread for every 6 people! That's the way it inevitably is in my house.

NEW ENGLAND
BOILED DINNER

6 pounds corned brisket of beef
1 medium turnip—quartered
5 small parsnips
6 small carrots
8 small onions
6 medium potatoes, peeled
1 medium cabbage, quartered and cored
6 beets

Cover meat with cold water and boil gently for 3 to 5 hours, until done. Skim the excess fat off the liquid. Add turnip, parsnips, carrots, onions and potatoes. Boil, uncovered, for 20 minutes. Add cabbage and continue cooking until the cabbage is soft. Place hot meat in a large platter. Surround it with the vegetables, including the beets which have been boiled separately.

Both horseradish and mustard are fine condiments to serve with this dish to "bring out the taste." Serves 6 to 8.

ROAST TURKEY

Stuff and truss the turkey. Place on its back in the roaster and lay a few strips of salt pork over the breast. Put into a very hot oven (500°) and after 30 minutes reduce the temperature to 375° and cover the roaster. Cook until tender. 20 to 25 minutes to the pound should be allowed. Plan on 1 pound of turkey for each guest, although most eat more.

Mrs. Richard Weld always bastes her turkey with currant jelly and 1 pint of brandy. Spoon this over the roasting turkey, a small amount at a time, often, during the time the turkey is roasting. One amateur I knew poured the whole amount over the turkey at once and the alcohol in the brandy blew the oven door off the hinges!!

CHESTNUT STUFFING

3 cups chestnut purée
1 cup soft bread crumbs
½ cup melted butter
1 tablespoon chopped parsley
1 tablespoon grated onion
½ teaspoon salt
⅛ teaspoon pepper
½ cup cream

To prepare the chestnut purée, boil a quart of large French chestnuts until tender. Remove shells and skins and rub through a sieve. Add bread crumbs, melted butter and seasonings. Add cream and mix lightly. Use with chicken and turkey.

TOAST STUFFING

8 slices toast
¼ cup butter, melted
2 cups hot milk
2 teaspoons poultry seasoning
1 teaspoon salt
1 tablespoon chopped onion
2 eggs, beaten

Cut toast into small cubes. Add melted butter, milk, seasonings and beaten eggs. Mix lightly but thoroughly.

ROAST CHICKEN

Stuff and dress the chicken and place on its back in a roasting pan. Rub with a paste of fat and flour to make the skin crisp and delicious. Put into a very hot oven (500°). After 15 or 20 minutes, when the skin is well seared, reduce the temperature to 375° and put cover on the roaster or add ½ cup water to the pan. Cook until tender, basting often with the liquid if an open pan is used. Make gravy in the pan. Plan on 1 pound of chicken for each person.

GRAVY

Pour off carefully all but 3 or 4 tablespoons of fat from the pan chicken was roasted in. Add 4 tablespoons flour and blend thoroughly. Add gradually 2 cups boiling water, stirring constantly, and cook until thickened. Season to taste with salt and pepper.

CRANBERRY SAUCE

1 quart cranberries
2 cups sugar

Pick over and wash berries. Add 2 cups water and cook until berries are tender. Add sugar and cook 5 minutes longer. Serves 8.

The cultivation of cranberries is one of the most important industries on Cape Cod. It is one of our earliest industries. The Pilgrim women learned from the Indians how to use them, and I am under the impression that more cranberries are grown here than anywhere else.

The harvesting time is an important time and a time of festival—a festival, of course, should be an important part of all harvests, and one is held annually in Plymouth now each autumn. Shops and houses are gaily decorated for the feast and

cranberry "rakes," which have long been antique collectors' items, are proudly placed on display.

The famous Toll House in Whitman has a Cranberry Room in which is displayed decoratively the Wakefield's extensive collection of these "rakes."

The autumn here, in my opinion, is our most beautiful time—except perhaps during our occasional snowfalls—and people drive from Boston and Providence and other cities and are impressed with the amethyst coloring of the cranberry bogs. They are very beautiful indeed.

CRANBERRY SHERRY JELLY

4 cups cranberries
2 cups white wine
2 cups sugar
pinch of salt
1 tablespoon lemon juice
1 cup sherry
2 envelopes gelatin

Bring the white wine to a boil, add the cranberries and simmer for ½ hour. Strain the juice from the cranberries through cheesecloth into another saucepan. Add sugar, salt, lemon juice and sherry, and simmer for a few minutes. Remove from fire and stir in the gelatin dissolved in ¼ cup cold water. When cool, pour into a quart mold. Chill on ice until firmly set. Then turn out onto a platter and garnish with whole cranberries and serve with turkey. Serves 8.

CRANBERRY MUFFINS

3 cups flour
3 tablespoons baking powder
1½ teaspoons salt
4 tablespoons sugar
1 teaspoon grated orange rind
½ cup shortening
1 egg, beaten
1 cup milk
1 cup fresh cranberries, chopped fine

Stir flour, baking powder, salt, sugar and orange rind in a good-sized mixing bowl. Cut in the shortening. Add the egg and milk, mixed together. Stir well. Fold in the cranberries. Bake in greased muffin pans in hot oven (425°) for 20 to 30 minutes. Should make 1 dozen muffins.

Laura Steton serves these at Sunday night suppers.

STEWED SQUASH
A LA NANTUCKET

Eliot Cary's grandmother always cooked squash this way on Nantucket. Her mother and her grandmother cooked it the same way before her. Eliot, dictatorially, says it is the only way to cook squash and it is tradition in his house with turkey—or any other roast:

Cut a large Hubbard squash into 6 pieces. Peel hard part off. Place in large skillet, tender side down. Cover with ⅓ part molasses, ⅔ part water. Stew uncovered for 1 hour. Turn shell side down. Continue to cook until tender. Serve hot. Serves 6.

ROAST VENISON

Wipe meat with a cloth wrung out in weak vinegar. Spread with melted butter. Sprinkle with salt. Cook in a hot oven (450°) for ½ hour. Reduce temperature to 350° for 20 minutes. Turn over when half done and dredge lightly with flour and salt. When flour begins to brown, spread meat with currant jelly and add a little water to the pan. Baste often. Serve hot with currant jelly. Plan on 1 pound for each person.

VENISON STEAK

Steaks should be about ½ inch thick. Sprinkle with salt and pepper, spread with melted butter. Broil like beefsteak, having the meat rare. Lay on a hot platter and spread with a mixture of ¼ cup butter, 2 tablespoons currant jelly, 2 tablespoons minced parsley, salt and pepper. Set in a hot oven (400°) for a moment.

WILD GRAPE JELLY

In our house Wild Grape Jelly is a "must" with venison.

Bring to a boil:

1 peck wild grapes
1 quart vinegar
½ cup cloves
½ cup cinnamon

and cook, just under the boiling point, until grapes are soft. Strain through a jelly bag. Boil the liquid 20 minutes. Add 6 pounds sugar. Boil until it jells, about 5 minutes. Should make 8 standard size jelly glasses.

CORN BREAD

1 cup sifted flour
4 tablespoons baking powder
½ teaspoon salt
2 tablespoons sugar
1 cup corn meal
4 tablespoons melted shortening
1 egg, well-beaten
1½ cups mik

Sift together flour, baking powder, salt and sugar. Add corn meal, shortening, well-beaten egg and milk to make a stiff batter. Transfer batter into a pan lined with waxed paper. Bake in a hot oven (400°) for 25 minutes. Serves 6.

INDIAN PUDDING

4 cups milk
½ cup yellow corn meal
2 tablespoons melted butter
½ cup molasses
1 teaspoon salt
1 teaspoon cinnamon
¼ teaspoon ginger
2 eggs

Scald milk. Pour slowly on corn meal, stirring constantly. Cook over hot water 20 minutes. Combine butter, molasses, salt, cinnamon and ginger. Beat eggs well; add with molasses mixture to corn meal. Pour into greased baking dish. Place in pan of hot water. Bake in moderate oven (350°) for 1 hour. Serve hot with hard sauce, plain or whipped cream, or vanilla ice cream. Serves 6.

BLUEBERRIES

Blueberries—both the high-bush variety and the low-bush—grow in great profusion on Cape Cod. Every Cape Cod child looks forward to the summer when he can go into the woods and pick them and sell them to the summer people. I used to often go with them years ago—and they were unforgettable days in the sunshine. When I taste blueberry jam even today the odor of pine needles in the hot sun, the tang of the sea breeze and the memory of dogs romping about us is very clear to me.

its fun to "go blueberrying"

The following recipes are for the ways the Cape Codders most frequently use blueberries—but a bowl of them with sugar and cream is unsurpassed, of course.

BLUEBERRY MUFFINS

2 cups pastry flour
3 teaspoons baking powder
½ teaspoon salt
½ cup sugar
2 eggs
¾ cup milk
4 tablespoons melted butter
1 cup blueberries

Mix and sift dry ingredients. Stir eggs, milk and butter and berries together, and mix with flour mixture. Spoon into muffin tins until about ¾ full. Bake about 20 minutes in hot oven (400°). Should make 1 dozen muffins.

PRESERVED
BLUEBERRIES

Cover ripe blueberries with water and swish them by hand to wash. Lift berries from water and place in a saucepan. Place wet berries on the fire and bring to a boil. (Add no water.) As soon as all the berries are boiling, remove from the fire. Lift the berries from the pan, taking very little liquid. Seal and store away in full, sterilized jars for future use, when berries are not in season.

Sweeten the remaining liquid with sugar and serve on sponge cake or shortcake. Garnish with whipped cream, if desired.

BLUEBERRY JAM

1½ quarts blueberries
2 tablespoons lemon juice
grated rind of ½ lemon
7 cups sugar

Boil rapidly for 2 minutes, skim several times if necessary. Fill and seal in sterilized glasses and store until winter.
Mrs. Cyrus McCormick's cook stews blueberries with gin. Delicious as a sauce for vanilla ice cream.

HOT SPICED
BLUEBERRY SAUCE

1 cup blueberries
¼ cup sugar
½ teaspoon cinnamon
¼ teaspoon nutmeg

Combine blueberries, sugar, cinnamon and nutmeg. Bring to boiling point; boil 5 minutes, stirring occasionally. Serve hot.
This sauce is delicious on ice cream.

BLUEBERRY DELIGHT

1 pint blueberries
½ cup whipping cream
1 banana
1 tablespoon powdered sugar
few grains nutmeg

Wash blueberries, place in individual serving dishes. Whip cream slightly. Peel banana, press through fine sieve. Add banana purée, sugar and nutmeg to cream. Pour over blueberries and serve. Serves 4.

BLUEBERRY CORNFLAKE PUDDING

1¼ cups crushed cornflakes
¼ teaspoon cinnamon
¼ cup sugar
2 tablespoons melted butter
2 cups blueberries

Combine cornflake crumbs, cinnamon, sugar and melted butter. Place 1 cup of berries in bottom of baking dish. Cover with ½ crumb mixture. Repeat. Bake in moderate oven (350°) 20 minutes. Serves 6.

BLUEBERRY WINE

1 quart blueberries
2 pounds sugar
1 pint grape juice
1 package seeded raisins
¼ yeast cake

Pour 4 cups boiling water over berries. Press out when cool enough to handle and pour liquid into a stone crock. Add sugar, grape juice, 2 cups lukewarm water, raisins and yeast. Let stand for 21 days. Then strain and bottle.

This wine is a favorite here and has been made for many generations by a great many of our best families.

STRAWBERRY JAM

The Cape is very famous for its rambling roses. They grow in dramatic profusion over the fences, walls, posts—and it is common to see them unchecked almost over the roofs of the low old houses—almost smothering them. Many people, those who can't come here often during the summer, wait until the ramblers are in bloom and visit us then.

Our soil is very sandy. But the great fogs alternating with days of intense hot sunshine do something for the roses that no other climate seems to be able to do.

I believe that goes for our strawberries, too. Everybody grows them with immense ease in the sandy soil of their backyards. I've even seen them growing along the railroad track at the edge of a dune in clear sand. Nobody knew how they got there—nobody tended them—but they survived two seasons until somebody else saw them and transplanted them to his backyard.

I could eat them every day of my life—picked fresh off the vines and dipped in powdered sugar, biting off the hulls; with sugar and cream; or made into jam.

Wherever I am they always make me think of Cape Cod, as the smell of the sea on the wind does or the odor of bayberries—and strawberry jam is so easy to make—everybody should have dozens of jars of it stored up—for winter breakfasts on hot buttered toast.

2 quarts strawberries
7 cups granulated sugar

Hull and wash the berries and crush them in a bowl, a layer at a time. Boil together with the sugar on a slow flame for perhaps 20 minutes until it "seems ready." By that I mean drop a spoonful onto a saucer and see if it is hardening. When it is, skim off the white foam, ladle it into sterilized jars, cover the tops with paraffin and store away until the snow flies. Should make 12 jars.

BEACH PLUM JELLY

I think it must be fun to have a Beach Plum Jelly stand. There are dozens of them on Cape Cod.

Mildred Crossman has one on the main highway where it crosses the dunes a few miles from my house. She is one of the jolliest souls I have ever met and we have become great friends. We hardly ever pass her house without dropping in for awhile to rest a bit in her kitchen. She's always boiling up Beach Plum Jelly.

When the berries are ready for picking—never ripe—it would be a bad day for Mildred if she couldn't be out on the dunes with all her children and their neighbors, day after day, picking them all over the valley. "I was a city girl once," she says, "and never knew anything that is as much fun as this.

"And the characters you meet when tending the stand!!"

This is her recipe. It is delicious served with chicken, lamb, or roast beef:

Wash and pick over red, unripe beach plums. Heat them to the boiling point in just enough water to cover. Drain. Then just cover them with boiling water. Cook until soft, mashing them from time to time. Extract juice and add 1 cup sugar to each cup juice. Boil mixture until it jells. Pour into sterilized jelly glasses. Cover with paraffin.

CHRISTMAS TREE GINGERBREAD

Gingerbread men, gingerbread women, gingerbread kings and queens, palaces, cottages, horses, carriages, hearts and flowers and stars—everything of gingerbread, and hung on the Christmas tree.

Don't bother with those "bought" cookie cutters. Cut your own designs with a sharp knife and have a wonderful time letting your imagination run riot.

Make crowns and hats and faces and buttons of raisins and walnuts and almonds and dried citron cut into amusing shapes.

christmas tree gingerbread

Draw hair and lace dresses and windows with a funnelled icing bag. And roses all over the roofs of the houses, and polka dots on the horses. It's a lot of fun making gingerbread people at Christmas time!

2¾ cups pastry flour
1 tablespoon baking powder
¼ teaspoon baking soda
1 teaspoon ground cloves
1 teaspoon ground ginger
1 scant tablespoon cinnamon
½ teaspoon salt
1 egg
¼ teaspoon allspice
1 cup brown sugar
⅔ cup dark molasses
½ cup butter

Sift flour into a bowl. Add baking powder, baking soda, cloves, ginger, cinnamon and salt. Sift all these ingredients again. In another bowl combine well-beaten egg, allspice, brown sugar, molasses and butter. Stir this liquid into flour mixture. Mix with your hands until flour has all been worked in. Divide the dough into 2 parts, rolling each into a ball. Roll out 1 ball on lightly floured board until ¼ inch thick. Flour top lightly, cut gingerbread designs with a sharp knife. Repeat with second ball of dough. Decorate with pieces of seedless raisins, candied fruits, citron, candies and nuts. Bake on greased baking sheet in oven (375°) for 12 minutes. Should make from 18 to 24 pieces.

Make a hole in each piece when it is baked but still hot and draw a silver ribbon through it to sparkle on your Christmas tree.

HOT FROSTED GINGERBREAD

½ cup strong hot coffee
½ cup butter
2 eggs
½ cup sugar
½ cup molasses
1½ cups flour
2 teaspoons baking powder
1 teaspoon ginger

Melt butter in hot coffee. Beat eggs, add sugar and molasses. Add to coffee mixture. Sift together flour, baking powder and ginger, to make a soft-drop batter. Spread batter ½ inch thick in a greased and floured dripping pan. Bake the gingerbread for 25 minutes in moderate oven (350°).

While the cake is still hot, frost it with this topping: Mix 1 cup confectioner's sugar with 4 tablespoons cream and flavor with vanilla. Cuts into 12 pieces.

DOUGHNUTS

1 cup milk
1 egg white
3 egg yolks
1 cup sugar
3 tablespoons melted butter
3½ cups flour (about)
4 teaspoons baking powder
1 teaspoon salt
½ teaspoon grated nutmeg

Let milk stand until it is at room temperature. Sift dry ingredients together. Beat eggs, add milk, sugar and melted butter. Add dry ingredients. Add enough additional flour to make dough just firm enough to roll but keep as soft as possible. Put ⅓ of mixture on floured board, knead slightly, pat and roll out ¼-inch thick. Shape with doughnut cutter. Fry in deep fat (370°). Drain on brown paper. Roll in powdered sugar when cool. Should make 2 dozen.

BASIC PIE CRUST PASTRY

2 cups pastry flour
½ teaspoon salt
⅓ cup butter
⅓ cup lard
ice water (about ⅓ cup)

Mix salt with flour. Work in butter and lard with finger tips until shortening is evenly mixed. Stir with fork and moisten dough with ice water. Pat gently into ball, chill thoroughly. Divide chilled pastry mixture into 2 portions, one slightly larger than the other. Chill larger portion until ready to roll out. Place smaller portion on slightly floured board. Roll with rolling pin into circle about 1 inch larger than pie tin and about ⅛ inch thick. Fold in half and lift into pie tin. Unfold and fit lightly into pan. Trim edge evenly with sharp knife, allowing about 1 inch extra around edge. (It is not necessary to grease pie plate.) Put in filling, heaping fruit high in center. Roll out reserved pastry in same way as for under crust. Brush edge of under crust with water. Fit top crust over filling, fold edge of top crust over under crust, press lightly together with fingers or tine of fork. Cut several slits near center to allow steam to escape during baking.

HOT RUM SAUCE

1 cup sugar
½ cup butter
¼ cup rum

Cook sugar in 1 cup water. When the syrup reaches the thread stage (230°), remove it from the fire. Add butter. When that has melted, stir in rum. Serve immediately with hot mince pie, or with any fruit soufflé or hot pudding.

MINCEMEAT

4 pounds lean beef
2 pounds beef suet
apples, quartered, cored
3 quinces, pared, cored
3 pounds sugar
2 cups molasses
2 quarts cider
3 pounds currants
4 pounds raisins, seeded, cut in pieces
½ pound finely-cut citron
1 quart grape juice
1 tablespoon cinnamon and mace
1 tablespoon powdered cloves
2 grated nutmegs
1 teaspoon pepper
salt to taste

Cover meat and suet with boiling water and cook until tender. Cool in water in which they are cooked; the suet will rise to top, forming a cake of fat, which may easily be removed. Chop meat fine and add it to twice the amount of finely chopped apples, Baldwins preferably. Add quinces, finely chopped, sugar, molasses, cider, currants, raisins and citron; also suet, and 1½ cups stock in which meat and suet were cooked. Heat gradually, stir occasionally, and cook slowly 2 hours. Then add grape juice and spices.

MINCE PIE

Make a double crust pie, using mincemeat as a filling. Bake in a hot oven until the pastry is browned, 30 minutes, (450° for 15 minutes, 350° for 15 minutes).

PUMPKIN PIE

2 cups cooked and strained pumpkin
2 teaspoons melted butter
½ teaspoon salt
1 cup sugar
½ teaspoon cinnamon
¼ teaspoon cloves
½ teaspoon mace
½ teaspoon ginger
1 cup milk
½ cup cream
2 eggs
pastry

Cook pumpkin very slowly until it is a golden brown. Add butter, salt, sugar, spices, milk, cream and well-beaten eggs. Pour into a pastry-lined pie plate. Bake in hot oven (450°) for 10 minutes, then reduce heat to moderate (350°) for 30 minutes. Bake until the filling is firm.

PUMPKIN CAKE

½ cup shortening
1 cup brown sugar
½ cup white sugar
1 egg
¾ cup cooked and strained pumpkin
2 cups flour
3 teaspoons baking powder
½ teaspoon cinnamon
½ teaspoon nutmeg
½ teaspoon ginger
½ teaspoon salt
⅔ cup chopped nuts
½ teaspoon soda
½ cup sour milk

Cream shortening and sugars together. Beat egg and add to pumpkin. Mix with creamed sugar and shortening. Sift flour, baking powder, spices and salt together. Mix nutmeats in flour mixture. Add soda to sour milk and add to the creamed mixture. Bake in loaf pan at 350° for 45 minutes.

SQUASH PIE

2 cups cooked squash
2 eggs
1 cup brown sugar
½ teaspoon salt
⅓ teaspoon mace
⅓ teaspoon ginger
¼ teaspoon cinnamon
2 cups rich milk
pastry

Press squash through a sieve. Beat eggs, add sugar, squash and remaining ingredients. Bake in a pastry-lined pie plate in hot oven (450°) for 10 minutes, then reduce to moderate oven (325°) for 30 minutes. Bake until filling is firm.

SQUASH CHIFFON PIE

1¼ cups squash
3 eggs, separated
½ cup brown sugar
⅔ cup milk
½ teaspoon ginger
½ teaspoon cinnamon
½ teaspoon nutmeg
½ teaspoon salt
1 tablespoon gelatin
3 tablespoons granulated sugar

Boil squash until tender and put through sieve. Add egg yolks, brown sugar, milk and seasonings. Cook in double boiler until custard consistency, stirring often. Soften gelatin in 3 tablespoons cold water and stir into hot custard. Cool. When mixture begins to thicken, fold in egg whites beaten stiff with the 3 tablespoons sugar.

APPLE PIE

6 to 8 sour apples
pastry
½ to ¾ cup sugar
¼ teaspoon grated nutmeg
¼ teaspoon salt
2 teaspoons lemon juice
few gratings lemon rind
½ tablespoon butter

Pare, core, and cut apples in eighths, put row around pastry-lined pie plate, ½ inch from edge, and work towards center until plate is covered; then pile on remainder. Mix sugar, nutmeg, salt, lemon juice, and grated lemon rind, and sprinkle over apples. Dot over with butter. Wet edges of under crust, cover with upper crust, and press edges together. Prick several places with fork.

"Off-Capers" Food

"Off-Capers"

Either you're a Cape-Codder or an "Off-Caper"!! It may be that there is such pride-in-place elsewhere, but it is rampant here. Your mother and your father may have been born here, you may have been born here—but your grandparents were not, or their parents were not, so you are just an "Off-Caper."

I've been here only thirty years but I always felt I belonged—now I'm sure of it. When I came back from Mexico last winter Bert Bangs said, "Peter, when you were down in those for'in parts I was trying to remember which house you were born in here—and by gosh, I can't remember!" That was one of the happiest days of my life.

Each season offers something for everyone to love and a reason to bring them here. I wonder if the superb fishing isn't perhaps the chief attraction. Everybody fishes—from the piers, from bridges, from boats and from the edge of the surf on the back shore, casting for stripers. The water is everywhere and all of it full of fish.

Antiquarians love Cape Cod, so do architects, artists, yachtsmen, young people, tired people and people who are escapists. It's a wonderful place for escapists—often we forget what day it is and seldom do we know the time. Few clocks here are ever correct.

Naturally all our diverse personalities have influenced the regional cooking—so I am including this group of recipes which I have enjoyed most from "Off-Capers" on Cape Cod.

SPAGHETTI AND GARLIC BREAD

Every Italian I have ever met assures me he, or she, can cook spaghetti better than and differently from any other

Italian. And I mean Italians in all walks of life, from bootblacks to opera singers and bearers of ancient titles. I'm sure that there is undoubtedly a subtle difference in each familiar recipe, but it is hard for me to find a great variance in the taste of the different braggarts' concoctions and I sincerely regret that it is so.

For several years I had the privilege of having an Italian brother-in-law. He was a young man and bore an ancient and honorable title. He loved America and was extremely happy here—except for the food, of course. We dined eventually in every Italian restaurant in New York and in a few of them, but very few, he found the food nostalgically good, but no one ever prepared spaghetti as it had been prepared in his own home in Naples. I became awfully self-conscious as I couldn't, for the life of me, find the subtle differences he found among them—to me some were good and some were not; that was all.

So for the sake of my cookbook and to avoid any arguments with my Italian friends, I prefer to use the basic recipe that Faith and John Cecil Holme use for their famous spaghetti parties in their house in Chatham.

After the excitement of the fabulous success of Cecil's play "Three Men on a Horse," he bought Faith a large old house on a hill overlooking the outer ocean, an hour's drive from my house. Often we would drive through the summer evening to dine on their terrace under the arbors, usually with interesting guests—often the casts from the Dennis Players or the Monomoy Theatre.

Faith makes wonderful spaghetti and always serves garlic bread with it. These are her recipes for them. We both agree that Portuguese bread is more delicious than French bread, but it is not easily obtained everywhere. Mr. Antone Brito makes wonderful bread, as he did in Portugal, in his tiny blue-and-white bakery down near the long wharf on Commercial Street. Don't miss it when you come to Provincetown.

ITALIAN SPAGHETTI

6 medium-sized onions, cut fine
1 clove garlic, chopped fine
1 large green pepper, cut fine
olive oil, sufficient to fry in
1 pound finely-ground round steak
1 large (quart size) can tomatoes
1 10-ounce can mushrooms
3 tablespoons dried mushrooms, chopped and soaked
2 drops Tabasco sauce
1 teaspoon Worcestershire sauce
salt and pepper to taste
1 package thin Italian spaghetti
grated cheese, to taste

Brown onions, garlic and green pepper to a golden brown in olive oil, very slowly. Add the ground meat and brown. Add tomatoes, after warming separately, and cook for ½ hour. Add mushrooms and seasonings and simmer sauce for ¾ hour, or until it is thick and has a well-blended flavor.

Cook 1 package spaghetti (long, thin Italian spaghetti), unbroken, in salted boiling water until tender, but still firm. Drain. Pour the sauce over spaghetti, which has been spread on a hot platter. Sprinkle with grated cheese before serving. Serves 8 to 10.

GARLIC BREAD

French bread, 1 loaf
garlic tip ends
¼ pound butter

Slice a loaf of French bread down to (but not all the way through) bottom crust. Bend bread to separate slices. Cut off tip ends of garlic, peel. Mash thoroughly. Cream crushed garlic with butter, spread between bread slices. Brush top of loaf with melted butter and put loaf on a tin in hot oven (400°). Bake about 10 minutes until heated through, brown on top. Break loaf apart and serve while hot in a napkin-covered basket.

peter hunt

Gull House Recipes

I shall always regret that Gull House has never reopened. It was a beautiful small inn, miles over the moors on a crisp autumn night, when we found it, closer to the Nauset Coast Guard Station than to anything else.

Jeanne and Bleecker Martin were wonderful hosts and built what one expects and seldom finds on Cape Cod: a grey shingled house with pine panels and huge fireplaces, chairs of great comfort, and superb food.

I was there only twice before it closed, but I shall always remember Brussels sprouts dipped in powdered almonds after they were boiled and buttered, and their cheese soup.

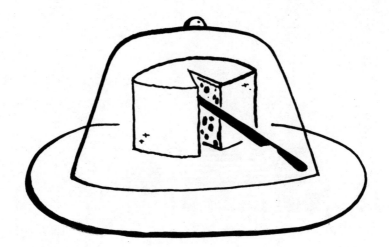

CHEESE SOUP

4 tablespoons butter
½ cup minced carrots
½ cup minced green peppers
½ cup minced onion
½ cup minced celery
⅓ cup flour
1 quart well-seasoned chicken stock
1 pound aged cheddar cheese, grated
3 cups milk
salt and pepper to taste

Melt butter in top of double boiler. Add vegetables and braise until tender. Do not brown. Blend in the flour. Add the stock and cook, stirring until thickened. Place over boiling water. Add cheese and cook until cheese has melted, stirring all the while. Add milk until consistency is that of cream. Season with salt and pepper. Serves 8 to 10.

LOBSTER BISQUE

1 5-pound lobster, boiled (or 2 2½-pound lobsters)
2 chicken bouillon cubes
1 onion, sliced
4 celery stalks, with leaves
1 bay leaf
2 whole cloves
8 whole peppers
4 tablespoons butter
4 tablespoons flour
3 cups milk
1 cup heavy cream
¼ teaspoon nutmeg
¼ teaspoon salt
parsley
paprika

Remove meat from lobster. Dice the meat and put aside.

Crush claws and shells. Place in a saucepan. Add 2½ cups water, bouillon cubes, onion, celery, bay leaf, cloves and peppers. Simmer for ½ hour and strain.

In another pan, melt butter. Stir in flour and slowly add milk, heavy cream, nutmeg and salt. When sauce is smooth and boiling, add slowly the strained stock and lobster meat. Simmer for 10 minutes. When serving, sprinkle with parsley and paprika. Serves 8 to 10.

CHICKEN NOEL

3 tablespoons butter
2 tablespoons flour
2 cups chicken broth, well seasoned
salt and pepper to taste
1 cup heavy cream
2 tablespoons sherry
3 cups boiled chicken meat
1 pound mushrooms, sliced and sautéd
1 pound sausage, cooked and sliced
½ cup almonds, blanched, shredded

Make sauce of butter, flour, chicken broth and salt and pepper to taste. When smooth, add heavy cream and sherry. Combine chicken, mushrooms and sausage in double boiler. Add sauce. Let simmer for 1 hour. Serve on spaghetti or rice. Sprinkle almonds on top. Serves 10 to 12.

BEEF STROGANOFF

4 pounds top round (beef)
½ pound butter
2 pounds mushrooms, sliced
2 large onions, chopped
2 tablespoons flour
2 cups beef consommé
2 tablespoons tomato juice
2 tablespoons vinegar
Worcestershire sauce
salt and pepper
paprika
1 pint sour cream

Slice steak into small, thin pieces, sauté them in half the butter (¼ pound).

In another pan, sauté mushrooms and onions in ¼ pound butter until onions are tender, but not browned.

Combine contents of both pans in a large double boiler. Sprinkle with flour, blend well. Add consommé, tomato juice and vinegar. Add Worcestershire sauce, salt, pepper and paprika to taste. Cook slowly for 1 hour. Add sour cream. Consistency should be like a thin cream sauce. Serves 12.

At Gull House this dish is served with steamed rice.

CIOPPINO SAUCE

¼ cup olive oil
¼ pound butter
6 cloves garlic, minced
4 large onions, finely chopped
2 green peppers, finely chopped
2 No. 8 cans stewed tomatoes, with juice
1 8-ounce can tomato paste
1 bottle chili sauce
2 No. 6 cans tomato sauce
1 teaspoon Worcestershire sauce
1 bay leaf
1 teaspoon chopped parsley
3 whole cloves
½ teaspoon saffron
½ teaspoon paprika
pinch of thyme
salt and pepper to taste
½ cup sherry
1 cup white wine
1 tablespoon grated orange rind

Sauté until tender in the olive oil and butter, the following ingredients: garlic, onions, green peppers. In large saucepan combine this mixture with the stewed tomatoes and juice: tomato paste, chili sauce, tomato sauce, Worcestershire sauce, bay leaf, parsley, cloves, saffron, paprika, thyme and salt and pepper to taste. Cook slowly for 3 hours. Stir occasionally. ½ hour before done, add sherry, white wine and grated orange rind. Makes enough sauce for 12 servings.

CIOPPINO FISH AND SHELLFISH

2 pounds striped bass or other flaky fish (cleaned, boned and cut in 2-inch pieces)
1 pint raw clams
1 pint raw oysters
1 pound small shrimp (cooked and cleaned)
1 pound cooked crabmeat
1 pint bay scallops, raw
4 1½-pound lobsters, boiled (split and claws cracked)
32 littleneck clams in shells (well scrubbed, but not cooked)
16 oysters in shell (cleaned but not cooked)

Place in layers the fish, raw clams, raw oysters, cooked shrimp, cooked crabmeat and raw bay scallops, in well-buttered individual casseroles. Place ½ lobster and 1 claw on top of each. Tuck 4 littleneck clams and 2 oysters around edges. Cover with a generous portion of Cioppino sauce. Bake in oven (375°) for 30 minutes, or until shellfish have opened. Serve with tossed salad and garlic toast. Serves 8.

INDIAN CURRY

Lee McCann and Gretchen Greene—neither of them come here any more. They never knew each other—it's a shame, they would have been great friends with great interests in common, although Lee told fortunes with cards, while Gretchen did it with tea leaves.

It seems now as if I always knew Gretchen. I think first in Coconut Grove when it was a tiny village before any of us grew up, and she had a tea room there and longed to go to China and India and Africa and Venice. So she went to China and met the Emperor and to India and had a houseboat on a lake in Kashmir and knew Rabindranath Tagore. She had a tea shop in Venice that was a constant tinkle of Venetian glass, and explored the whole world with Gertrude Hoffman later and wrote a book all about it called *The Whole World and Company*. She loved Indian food and loved to prepare it.

Lee was always happy when we would give a party and ask her to cook for it, because she delighted to make Indian Curry. In those days I lived in an old boathouse that hung over the harbor practically on stilts and it was sparsely furnished.

Lee would arrive in the late afternoon with hampers of Chinese bowls filled with shredded coconut and chopped peanuts and chutney and Bombay Duck and French fried onion rings and hard-boiled eggs chopped fine, the whites in one bowl, the yolks in another, and sliced cucumbers marinated in vinegar. These are the condiments that one always sprinkles lavishly over the curry dish on one's plate.

And this is the way Lee wrote down for me her method of preparing Indian Curry:

    1 pound lean beef
    1 tablespoon flour
    3 large onions, cut fine
    1 sprig of parsley
    1 teaspoon salt
    3 dashes black pepper
    2 tablespoons drippings
    1 tablespoon ginger
    1 tablespoon curry powder
    ½ pint tomato sauce

Cut beef into pieces 1 inch square. Dredge these with flour. Put drippings into a frying pan, and when pan is very hot add meat. Shake and stir until nicely browned. Add flour and 4 cups boiling water. Stir until it boils. Add onion, finely cut, and parsley. Cover and simmer 2 hours. Add salt and freshly-ground black pepper when half cooked. Shortly before the meat is thoroughly cooked, cut 2 large onions very fine and fry in a saucepan with a little fat and ginger. Add curry powder, stir until light brown. Add meat to this, and cook for 15 minutes. Add tomato sauce and cook 15 minutes more. Serves 4.

Serve over perfectly cooked rice—and, to me, rice should always be cooked perfectly—otherwise it is no good at all. In fact, it is then a horrible thing. And it is easy to cook rice perfectly; it is merely a matter of cooking it in plenty of constantly bubbling water until it is just tender but not mushy. Drain it instantly in a colander and pour boiling water through it. This removes the loose starch. Let it steam for a few minutes and it will be perfect, with each grain separate, as it should be.

My memory of these parties is always that they were in the early autumn with a tang in the air and a wind would

make the waves swish under the boathouse. That part I may be wrong about now. But the food I'll never forget.

LENTIL SOUP

Bruce McKain is a famous artist.

He is a large, happy man who beams all the time.

He is happiest when he is painting snow scenes when the snow is slush on the streets of Provincetown.

He beams broadest when he comes in out of the cold and his wife, Amy, has lentil soup hot on the stove for him.

This is how Amy wrote out her recipe for me:

    1 cup lentils
    ham bone
    4 medium potatoes, sliced
    4 carrots, sliced
    2 medium onions, sliced
    1 green pepper, sliced
    1 bay leaf
    pinch of marjoram
    1 teaspoon Worcestershire sauce
    salt and pepper to taste

Put lentils and ham bone in 8 cups water in pressure cooker. Add potatoes, carrots, onions, green pepper and seasonings. Cook 20 minutes under 15 pounds pressure. Let cooker cool by itself. Remove ham from bone. If pressure cooker is not used, cook according to time given on lentil package. Serves 10 to 12.

One day this winter Bruce and I were in North Truro and we stopped in at the Tom Blakemans' out of the cold.

Marion gave us each a bowl of lentil soup which she had just made.

Bruce beamed then, too.

This is how Marion Blakeman makes it:

2½ cups lentils
7 quarts water
3 tablespoons salt
½ teaspoon red pepper
½ cup parsley
2 cups celery, cut fine
2 cups carrots, cut fine
2 cups onions, cut fine
ham bone, turkey or chicken carcass

Soak lentils in enough water to cover overnight. Add remaining water and other ingredients. Cook over low heat for 3 hours. Serves 15 to 20.

Both are wonderful. Try a bowl at mid-morning on a cold winter's day.

My mother always serves it to us on Saint Patrick's day for lunch. She spikes it slightly with dry sherry as if it were Black Bean Soup.

MARY BICKNELL'S PEA SOUP

Mary Bicknell for years, even before I came to Provincetown, has been one of the most famous hostesses of all our town.

As a young boy I had been brought up on the books of F. Hopkinson Smith with his glamorous pictures of artists of that period, and *Trilby* and *La Vie de Boheme*. I pictured then an artist's studio as a romantic place set apart from the rest of the world. Thirty years ago when I first came to Provincetown the Bicknell's place seemed all of that to me. I think W. H. W. Bicknell, the world-famous etcher, Mary's husband, was perhaps the first artist I had ever met.

Bick's studio was a long converted fishhouse, jutting into the water, one end used as a studio in which the huge etching press predominated. They knew everybody and the walls were covered with paintings and cartoons of his friends. There were so many of these mementos that many of them were stacked on the floor and leaning against the walls.

Mary loved the theatre and had organized the "Wharf Players" here which was world famous. She was a superb actress and played in many of the plays. Theatre people with their fabulous sense of humor were always in and out of the studio.

The whole town seemed to come to them for cocktails and stay on for an impromptu dinner, after which maybe a string quartet would assemble and play long into the night. Their hospitality was so great that often it would be dawn before we left.

Mary now lives alone across the street from me. I told her how anxious I was to include her pea soup recipe in this book as it is so distinctive from any other pea soup. She laughed and said, "Of course you can't 'bake five beans'—and so you can't make a little pea soup—just enough for one person. So that's why I'm always sending it to my neighbors when I make a bowl of it for myself."

And, like all good cooks, it was hard to learn from her the exact measurements—good cooks constantly say, "a small bowl of this; use your judgment about how much of that." But yesterday we brought Mary over to my house and cooked her favorite soup under her directions, and in this way pinned down the exact proportions of all the ingredients:

2 cups ("one small bowl" as Mary says) full of sliced onions fried in simmering sausage fat
1 pound dried green peas
2 quarts water
1 teaspoon whole peppercorns
4 whole cloves
scant teaspoon dried mustard
3 long slices bacon, cut fine with kitchen shears
1 cup celery stalks, diced

Cook very slowly for 2 to 3 hours. Add a pinch of oregano after 2 hours. (This is because the flavor of this herb is lost if cooked too long, Mary tells us.) Then simmer for another hour. Serve with croutons.

As we made this fine soup we found that it was necessary to occasionally add another cup of water, as it often would thicken almost to a paste. As Mary says, "Be guided by the consistency." I wouldn't be surprised if, by the time the soup was finished, we had used at least 6 quarts of water, cup by cup, during the cooking to arrive at the consistency of a thick soup and not a heavy paste. Serves 12.

The Southward Inn

An inn, especially a Cape Cod inn, should be old, mellow, furnished with antiques, not too large, with rooms on many levels with a few steps between them, and should have a parrot that some seafaring gentleman left many years ago. It should have two bars, one where everyone likes to sit and talk with the fishermen and perhaps dance a square dance on Friday nights when the man who plays the fiddle comes around. Then there must, nowadays, be a Cocktail Lounge. But it could be furnished with Victorian chairs and upholstered benches and the marble-topped tables should be cut low, down to coffee table height, and the lights could be mellow to flatter and please the guests who like to dress for dinner.

These people would naturally dine in the dining room with the crystal chandeliers and the damask draperies.

The rest of us, of course, would be happier in the huge beamed-ceiling room with the coppers hanging from the rafters and the primitive paintings and the "coaching" prints and the brick bar, with the beaming barmaid behind it.

As I re-read this it all seems to me as if I remembered it all from a novel laid in the English countryside rather than Cape Cod. But actually it inadequately describes the Southward Inn, directly across from my house in Orleans. I imagine that house and mine were perhaps built at the same time and by the same architect, and its elms which abut mine were planted as one row —their age is the same.

The Inn was unquestionably the great house of the town, with its stables and carriage houses which have been gradually incorporated into one building under one roof of many angles and gables and turrets, which gives a most entertaining outline to the landscape from my windows across the highroad.

And, like all fine Inns, I have found the Southward Inn a bulwark of hospitality. I stop in the bar during the snow for a hot buttered rum and they fuss because a cold is beginning in me. "It's a shame you should sleep in your own draughty house when we have some empty rooms." So, firmly and with kindness, and without too much resistance on my part, I'm put to bed in a canopy bed in a room with a fine view of the cove; and fruit juices and broths are brought to me until my cold has run its course.

Or, if I give a party, they know of it and send me silver trays of canapés to make it all gayer; and once, during the summer, while people were having drinks on my terrace during the full moon, the owner sent a violinist and a man with an accordion to make music for my guests.

I thank you indeed, Mrs. Eve Rich, for having such a lovely Inn across the road from me.

And I thank you for your chef. He has allowed me to publish the following recipes from his kitchen. I think these are the dishes I order more than any in your Inn:

ONION SOUP

3 large onions
⅓ cup olive oil
¼ cup sweet butter
1½ quarts boiling beef stock
1 scant teaspoon sugar
1 tablespoon butter
1 small clove garlic
Parmesan cheese
Cayenne pepper

Peel onions and slice them very thin, separating the rings. Heat oil, add onion rings and cook very, very slowly over a gentle flame. When onions begin to get transparent, add sweet butter and continue cooking, over a low flame, until the onion

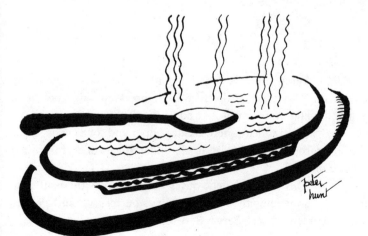

rings are limpid. Do not season. Add boiling stock and sugar, stirring the liquid gradually into the transparent onion rings, and continue to stir gently from the bottom of the pan, until the mixture comes to a boil. Add 1 tablespoon butter and 1 garlic clove, chopped fine. Lower the heat and let simmer very gently for 15 minutes. Serve with toasted bread, placed in the soup bowl just before serving. Sprinkle generously with grated Parmesan cheese and a dash of Cayenne pepper. Serves 10 to 12.

CODFISH IN SOUR CREAM

2 pounds fresh codfish, in one piece
1 bay leaf
1 slice lemon
2 cloves
2 tablespoons olive oil
4 green onions, cut fine
1 teaspoon minced parsley
1 large tomato
1 cup sour cream
pinch of marjoram
pinch of sweet basil
salt and pepper

Wrap the fish, together with the bay leaf, lemon and cloves in cheesecloth to keep it from breaking, and cook it in gently boiling water until it is done. Cook the onions in the oil, add the parsley, tomato, herbs, salt, pepper and sour cream. Pour this over the fish and heat it all under the broiler for just a minute or two.

This we find delicious when served with small new potatoes seasoned with minced parsley, butter, salt and pepper and grated lemon peel. Serves 8 to 10.

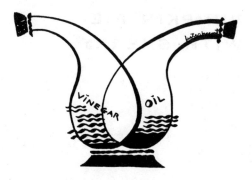

WATER CRESS
AND BEET SALAD

15 medium-sized beets
beet juice
French dressing
1 large clove garlic
1 medium-sized onion
2 large bay leaves
3 whole cloves
1 teaspoon celery seeds for each cup dressing
salt and pepper
dash of Cayenne
water cress

Cut off top of beets, leaving an inch of stem on to prevent bleeding. Wash beets and bake in moderate oven (350°) until soft when tested with fork. Rub off the skins. Cut off stems and let beets cool. Slice beets thinly into a mixing bowl, let stand for ½ hour. Drain juice and add to it ⅔ its amount in French dressing, clove garlic (gently bruised), onion (finely chopped), bay leaves, whole cloves, celery seeds, salt, pepper and dash of Cayenne. Let dressing stand overnight. In the morning drain through a sieve. Pour over sliced beets. Serve thoroughly chilled. Garnish with crisp fresh water cress. Serves 6 to 8.

PUMPKIN PIE
WITH SHERRY

1 pumpkin, sieved
milk
maple sugar
eggs
1 tablespoon butter for each cup pumpkin
cinnamon
cloves
ginger
nutmeg
salt
½ cup sherry

Cut pumpkin in half, crosswise. Remove the seeds. Scoop out the meat of the pumpkin, leaving a good solid shell of the lower half. Steam the scooped-out pumpkin meat in a double boiler until it is tender. Press it through a fine sieve. Measure sieved pumpkin into a large bowl and add an equal amount milk and half as much maple sugar. Beat egg and 1 tablespoon butter for each cup pumpkin. Season to taste with cinnamon, cloves, ginger, nutmeg and salt. Add ½ cup sherry, more or less according to your taste. Beat the mixture until it is very light and creamy. Pile it into the lower half of the pumpkin shell. Place the stuffed shell in a hot oven (400°) for 10 minutes, then lower the heat to 300° and bake until the top is brown and shiny.

A very festive autumn dish that never fails to delight the clientele. Serves 8 to 10.

MARY CORDEIRO'S
BIRTHDAY CAKES

Ever since we've known Mary—and it's been over ten
years now, she has made a cake for all our birthdays. Sometimes
we are tempted to slide in a few extra birthdays just for the sake
of the cake:

BIRTHDAY CAKE

4 eggs
½ teaspoon cream of tartar
3 tablespoons cold water
1½ cups sugar
½ cup boiling water
1½ cups flour
1 teaspoon baking powder
¼ teaspoon salt
1 teaspoon vanilla

Beat egg whites with cream of tartar until stiff. Then beat egg yolks with 3 tablespoons cold water for 3 minutes. Gradually add sugar and ½ cup boiling water. Beat until frothy. Add flour mixed with baking powder and salt. Add vanilla. Then fold in egg whites, beaten. Bake 1 hour in slow oven (300°).

ICING

1 pound confectioner's sugar
juice of ½ orange (about)
2 tablespoons melted butter

Blend sugar and melted butter in shallow bowl with a fork. Add orange juice as needed to make icing smooth enough to spread.

MARY CORDEIRO'S CHOCOLATE CAKE

Several times, usually on a gray day, Mary has dropped in unexpectedly with a chocolate cake. "It seemed such

a gray day I thought I'd make you a cake for tea." This is the recipe for that cake:

3 squares bitter chocolate
1 tablespoon butter
1 tablespoon shortening
3 eggs
1½ cups sugar
1½ cups flour
1½ teaspoons baking soda
¼ teaspoon salt
1½ cups cream
1 cup chopped walnut meats
1 teaspoon vanilla

Melt chocolate in double boiler with butter and shortening. Beat eggs, add sugar to eggs and beat together. Add melted chocolate, beat. Sift dry ingredients together. Add to chocolate mixture, alternating with cream. Mix chopped nuts in a little flour, add to cake mixture, stir. Next stir in the vanilla. Bake in medium oven (350°) for 45 minutes.

ICING

3 squares bitter chocolate
1 tablespoon butter
1 tablespoon shortening
1 pound confectioner's sugar
½ cup cream
½ teaspoon vanilla

Melt chocolate, butter and shortening in double boiler. Remove from heat. In same pan blend in sugar and cream until icing is smooth enough to spread. Stir in vanilla.

Frank Lee's Recipes

FRIED MUSHROOMS

Frank Lee is very famous for the intricate enamels he bakes on copper. To us he is as famous for his dinner parties and for his birthday presents. Both his parties and his birthday presents are the most elaborate imaginable. People always say, "But, Frank, how do you get the time?" and his answer is, "It's fun, just fun," which bears out my contention that if a thing is fun to do, it is easy to do.

My Mother always says she never can have enough mushrooms. So Frank always brings her "enough" on her birthday.

Arranged on a huge toll tray were rows and rows of mushrooms for her party.

While he was picking mushrooms he found a small abandoned bird's nest which he used in the center of the tray and filled it with halved boiled eggs stuffed with chopped mushrooms.

Surrounding the bird's nest were rows of mushrooms on small circlets of toast. One row of toast flavored with anchovy paste, one row flavored subtly with crushed olives. Another row had the mushrooms chopped coarsely and sprinkled over liver paté. A row of large mushrooms were left whole.

The whole tray was edged with small white chrysanthemums. No birthday present could have been gayer to please a mushroom lover.

Frank Lee tells us that his "secret" of preparing mushrooms for hors d'oeuvres is to fry them in olive oil and when you take them from the pan, squeeze fresh garlic juice on them with a garlic crusher.

When we asked him how much garlic juice, again, like all good cooks, he said, "You just have to use your own judgment."

After many of the parties at the Lee House in North Truro I would stay behind after the rest of the guests left until Frank had written out for me the ingredients of a dish I especially enjoyed that evening.

The following are six of these recipes in Frank's own words (he is an individualist, you will notice, of course):

STUFFED MUSSELS

Bring in a huge tray of stuffed mussels and watch their eyes pop!

Boil and drain a cup of rice. Mix 2 tablespoons capers with it (if salted, rinse salt off first) and 1 tablespoon hot Hungarian paprika. If your paprika is not hot enough, add enough red pepper to make the rice just faintly tasting of "heat." Make your own garlic salt by rubbing a clove of garlic into a teaspoon of salt in a wooden mortar and pestle until a paste results. Add this to the rice mixture. Now steam open about 3 quarts of mussels by keeping the lid on the pan until their shells open enough for you to get a tablespoon in. Insert into the shell, over the mussel, a tablespoon of the rice and close the shell on it. Arrange all the stuffed mussels in a large baking pan and pour a small stream of olive oil over all. Broil slowly for about 20 minutes and let them stand in the broiler with the heat off for 20 minutes more. This seasons them, and when you serve them they will be just warm enough for eating. Serves 6 to 8.

You will wish you had made more.

CHOP HOUSE LAMB

The day before you invite the Boss home to dinner, bribe your butcher to obtain for you a *4" piece* of the center of loin of heavy mutton. Broil at least 20 minutes all in one piece and serve *one of these hunks of lamb for each person.*

You need only fresh peas with this, it is the *very best* of food.

One of the best reasons for anyone to live on Cape Cod, is that they may be near the World's Paramount Hangover Cure at all times, the Prairie Oyster.

PRAIRIE OYSTER

With a small glass in your shaking hand, pour into it about a teaspoon of good vinegar and knock a shell-less egg into it. Add a sprinkle of Worcestershire sauce, and salt and pepper over all.

Upsidaisy.

If one's good, two's better.

RADISHES AND ONIONS
AND SOUR CREAM

The most beautiful lunch on earth is this dish. It's very simple:

Cut up several red radishes and several small green onions into a pretty bowl. You're going to eat out of this bowl.

Plump over this a pint of sour cream. That is absolutely all, nothing else.

Eat it with a spoon.

MIDNIGHT BOOGEY—
NEVER BEFORE 12!

With your left hand flap 2 slices of bread with their centers cut out into a big iron spider which is sizzling hot from butter.

With your right hand break 1 egg each into the holes in the bread. In a moment or so the bread is pan-toasted and the eggs fried on one side, too.

With your right hand wielding a spatula, flip the boogeys over and with your left hand pour store-bought chili sauce over the turned-up egg center.

When the bread is toasted on both sides, the chili sauce will be warmed through.

Slide the Boogeys onto a plate and dig in with a fork, from the egg outwards.

Make everybody left at the party one of these, and be prepared to continue.

PISSALADIERA

Buy and rush home with 2 pounds of fresh French-type dough from your local foreign bakery. Spread this out about ½-inch thick on a big cookie sheet or pan and let rise in a warm place, the edges a little thicker than the center.

When you wish to bake it, which takes only 20 minutes before eating, pour over the dough a purée of onions lightly but long sautéd in olive oil, perhaps 2 pounds of onions.

Spread over this crushed black olives and wisps of anchovies and, if you like, tomato purée, the latter optional. If you use tomato, use a more than liberal toss of basil in the purée.

Pour a nice amount of olive oil in a thin stream over this, hurry and stick it in the oven (350°).

When done (20 minutes) and lightly browned, cut in pie-shaped wedges and eat with the fingers as an hors d'oeuvre *de luxe*. Serves 6 to 8.

PARTY BREADS FROM OVER THE BORDER—SOPAIPILLAS

Into 4 cups of flour sifted with 4 teaspoons of baking powder, cut ¼ cup pure fat, 2 teaspoons salt and enough water to hold all this together.

Roll thin and cut in harlequins, fry in deep hot lard. Serves 6 to 8.

These will raise any dinner into the party class.

FRANCES EULER'S RECIPES

Just before Reeves and Frances Euler flew to Mexico to paint, this winter, I pinned Frances down long enough to give me the three following recipes which are unique in our part of the country:

RED PEPPER JAM

4 cups chopped hot red peppers
salt
3 cups sugar
1½ cups vinegar

Sprinkle a little salt over the peppers after they have been chopped and let stand 3 hours. Add sugar and vinegar and cook until thick. Don't allow to get dark red. If too juicy, add a little minute tapioça. Excellent with roast beef. Should fill 8 pint jars.

Warning: Be sure to use rubber gloves, hot peppers burn the skin.

RAW CRANBERRY RELISH

1 package cranberries
1 large unpeeled orange
1 large unpeeled apple
1 cup unsalted nuts
¾ cup brown sugar

Wash and dry fruits. Grind everything. Add sugar and chill before serving.

Very good for buffet suppers.

MARINATED MUSHROOMS

Wash fresh mushrooms with a damp cloth, trim off the bottom of the stems and slice very thin. Place in a bowl a layer of mushrooms, a layer of raw onions sliced thin, a layer of chopped parsley (cut with scissors). Sprinkle with salt. Repeat until the required amount you want is arrived at. Pour oil and diluted vinegar over this mixture. Toss well, add more oil and vinegar and toss again. Put in ice box for 3 hours, or until wilted. Mix well before serving as a canapé or as a salad. ½ pound of mushrooms makes a nice amount for 6 as a canapé. ¼ pound makes salad for 2.

PICKLED MUSHROOMS

Lytton Buehler hated to cook; he wouldn't and couldn't cook anything—but mushrooms. He was one of the first painters I ever met. Painting and talking about art filled his whole life. But mushrooms rivaled art to him. This is his recipe for pickling them:

Simmer for 16 minutes:

2 cups vinegar
1 cup sugar
6 peppercorns
½ teaspoon salt
1 teaspoon mustard seeds
1 teaspoon celery seeds
1 bay leaf
3 cloves

Add 24 mushrooms, stemmed but not peeled, and simmer slowly until they are soft enough to be easily pierced with a toothpick. Remove the mushrooms from the pickle to a sterilized glass jar and pour the syrup over them. They will keep indefinitely but they are ready to serve as soon as they are cold. Should fill 2 jars.

STUFFED MUSHROOMS

Food consumes Louise Frank's Elspeth completely. It colors her entire outlet on life. Delightfully she transmutes everything she sees into terms of food.

Once I asked her why she went each year to Colorado Springs for her vacation.

"It is so beautiful there—the snow-capped mountains are just like meringues!"

That's Elspeth. She is happiest when there are many house guests who stay for a long time and she can bedazzle them with dishes that are involved in their making:

> 3 pounds mushrooms
> juice of one lemon
> 3 chicken livers
> ¼ pound chopped beef
> 1 boiled egg, chopped fine
> ½ onion, browned in butter
> 2 celery stalks chopped fine
> salt and pepper
> paprika

Peel and stem the mushrooms and boil them in salt water and the lemon juice. Remove from the fire as soon as the water boils. Pick over the mushrooms and set the large ones aside. Chop the small ones, adding the stems, and mix well with the rest of the ingredients, season, and spread a heaping layer of this stuffing in each large mushroom. Bake (350°) until the mushrooms are tender—about ½ hour. Serve on rounds of thin, hot buttered toast at luncheon. Should serve 8.

MUSHROOMS COOKED IN SOUR CREAM

Another one of Elspeth's methods of preparing mushrooms, served as a vegetable with the meat course:

1 onion, chopped
6 tablespoons butter
flour
2 tablespoons milk
1½ pounds mushrooms, sliced
salt and pepper
¾ pint sour cream

Brown the onions in the butter, sprinkle with flour, stir until brown; add the milk gradually. Bring to a boil and add the sliced mushrooms. Season with salt and pepper, simmer. Add ½ of the sour cream and cook very gently until the mushrooms are tender. Stir in the rest of the sour cream. Serve immediately after it is heated. Serves 6.

PICKLES

Washington Irving wrote a wonderful description of the activities in an early Knickerbocker kitchen which I have never forgotten, although it is at least twenty-five years since I have read it. Each autumn here I feel as if I were actually alive in the scene he so carefully detailed. Every Cape Cod house-

wife enjoys herself, I feel, during September and October more than at any other time of the year. Her sense of accomplishment must be tremendous as she preserves for the long winter months ahead.

SLICED CUCUMBER PICKLES

24 medium-sized cucumbers
12 onions
1 quart vinegar
2 cups sugar
1 tablespoon turmeric
2 teaspoons celery seed
2 teaspoons mustard seed

Wash, clean and slice cucumbers. Peel and slice onions. Soak sliced cucumbers and onions 2 hours in a brine, made of 1 cup salt and 8 quarts water. Drain. Combine vinegar, sugar, turmeric, celery seed and mustard seed and bring to a boil. Add cucumbers and onions. Boil 10 minutes. Pack into hot, sterilized jars. Seal at once. Should fill 12 quart jars.

SWEET CUCUMBER PICKLES

30 small cucumbers
1 quart vinegar
1 cup sugar
2 teaspoons whole black pepper
1 teaspoon grated horseradish
1 3-inch stick cinnamon
¾ teaspoon mustard seed
½ teaspoon whole cloves

Wash and drain cucumbers. Cover with brine, made by adding 1 cup salt to 1 gallon water. Let stand 24 hours. Drain, rinse in fresh water, drain again, and cover with vinegar mixed with sugar and spices. Bring to a boil and simmer for 3 minutes. Fill sterilized jars to overflowing. Seal at once. Should fill 10 quart jars.

DILL PICKLES

36 cucumbers
dill
garlic
2 cups vinegar
¾ cup salt

Wash cucumbers. Pack into hot, sterilized jars with pieces of dill. Add a clove of garlic to each jar. Boil 3½ quarts water, 2 cups vinegar and ¾ cup salt for 5 minutes. Pour hot over cucumbers, filling jars to ½ inch from top. Seal at once. Should fill 8 quart jars.

MUSTARD PICKLES

20 medium cucumbers, sliced
2 small heads cauliflower, separated into flowerets
6 green peppers, diced
1 cup salt
8 cups sugar
1¼ cups dry mustard
1 cup flour
½ ounce turmeric
1 quart vinegar
1 quart tiny onions
2 quarts green tomatoes, cut into pieces

Place cucumbers and cauliflower in container and sprinkle with salt. Let stand overnight. Mix sugar, mustard, flour and turmeric. Add vinegar and 4 cups water and bring to a boil. Add peppers, onions and tomatoes and cook until tender and sauce has thickened. Seal in hot, sterilized jars. Should fill 8 quart jars.

MIXED PICKLES

2 cups pickling onions
1 quart small cucumbers
4 tablespoons white mustard seed
4 tablespoons salt
1 cup sugar
1 quart cider vinegar
2 cups carrots, cut into 2-inch pieces
2 red peppers, seeds removed
2 cups celery, cut into 2-inch pieces

Cover onions and cucumbers, in separate containers, for 24 hours with brine, made with 1 cup salt to 4 quarts water. Drain. Soak in cold water 2 hours, and drain again. Mix onions and cucumbers. Add spices, salt, sugar, and vinegar; let stand overnight in covered pan. Drain off liquid and heat it. Add carrots and celery and simmer for 15 minutes. Put onions and cucumbers in hot, sterilized jars, pour over liquid and seal. Should fill 8 quart jars.

GREEN TOMATO PICKLES

1 peck green tomatoes, sliced
12 onions, sliced
1½ ounces black pepper
1 ounce whole allspice
¼ pound ground mustard
1 ounce whole cloves
1 ounce mustard seed
½ cup salt
1 quart vinegar

Arrange tomatoes and onions in layers in a pan. Sprinkle salt between layers. Let stand overnight. Drain. Add other ingredients. Cover with vinegar and simmer gently for 15 minutes. Pack into hot, sterilized jars. Seal at once. Should fill 8 quart jars.

BREAD AND BUTTER PICKLES

25 medium cucumbers, sliced
12 onions, sliced
½ cup salt
2 cups sugar
2 teaspoons turmeric
2 teaspoons cassia buds
1 quart vinegar
2 teaspoons mustard seed
2 teaspoons celery seed

Soak cucumbers and onions in ice water with salt for 3 hours. Combine all other ingredients and heat to boiling. Add drained cucumbers and onions and heat for 2 minutes. Do not allow to boil. Pour into sterilized jars and seal at once. Should fill 8 quart jars.

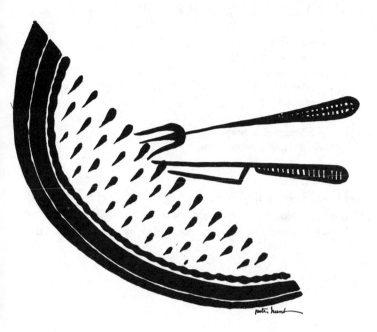

PICKLED WATERMELON

3½ pounds watermelon rind
2½ pounds sugar
1½ cups cider vinegar
¼ teaspoon oil of cloves
¼ teaspoon oil of cinnamon

Remove outer skin from watermelon rind and cut into thin, even slices. Soak overnight in brine made of ½ cup salt and 8 cups water. Drain, cover with cold water and cook gently for 1½ hours. Drain well. Boil together sugar, vinegar, oil of cloves and oil of cinnamon for 10 minutes. Add cooked rind. Bring slowly to boiling point. Remove from fire. Let stand overnight. Reheat for 3 days. After reheating last time, pour into hot, sterilized jars. Seal at once. Should make 6 pints.

PICKLED BEETS

2 cups cider vinegar
1 teaspoon salt
2 cups sugar
1 tablespoon white mustard seed
1 teaspoon allspice
1 teaspoon cloves
1 tablespoon cinnamon
small whole cooked beets

Combine vinegar, 2 cups water, salt, sugar and spices (which have been tied in a muslin bag. Use whole spices). Boil for 5 minutes. Skin beets and add. Simmer 15 minutes. Remove spice bag. Fill sterilized jars and seal. Should fill 6 quart jars.

QUICHE

John Stevens, until he left here, was a one-dish man. Often he would drop in upon us on late winter afternoons and if it was Mary's day off he'd stay and make quiche, the only dish he knew how to make. Incidentally, he made it superbly:

2 cups pastry flour
¼ pound butter
1 egg yolk
1 pinch salt
¼ cup ice water

Work the above into a dough and chill in the icebox for ½ hour. Roll out the dough and line the bottom of a pie pan with it.

FILLING

2-3 slices boiled ham, diced
4-6 large onions
1 tablespoon butter
6 thin slices Swiss cheese
4 eggs
pinch salt
dash Cayenne
pinch nutmeg
2 cups milk

Sprinkle over pie shell the cooked ham—2 or 3 slices, diced—then a layer of sliced onions which have been sautéed in a tablespoon of butter until soft but not browned. John usually used four good-sized onions and a tablespoon of butter but we have found that six sautéed onions have pleased some of our guests' palates even more than when we used four. Add 6 thin slices of swiss cheese. Then beat in a saucepan 4 eggs, a

pinch of salt, a dash of Cayenne and a pinch of nutmeg. Beat into this 2 cups of hot milk. Heat over a low flame and continue beating until the custard begins to thicken. Pour this into the pie shell and cook in a moderate oven (350°) until the custard is set. It should be a golden-brown color. Serve piping hot, cut into pie slabs directly from the pan. Serves 6.

This, with a glass of red wine, followed by black coffee is wonderful after skiing.

CHICKEN AND WINE

My father stood by the old saw that there was just one way of doing anything—meaning the right way, of course. But we have found that there are three ways, at least, of cooking chicken in wine; and all of them are good ways:

ONE

1 young frying chicken (3 or 3½ pounds)
3 tablespoons fat for frying
¾ teaspoon salt
¼ teaspoon pepper
12 small white onions
12 medium-size mushrooms
1 clove garlic
1 No. 1 can tomatoes
1½ cups stock
½ cup white wine

Cut the chicken into serving pieces. Brown in the fat. Add seasoning, onions, mushrooms, garlic and tomatoes. Cover frying pan and cook in moderate oven (350°) about 1½ hours. While cooking, add 1 cup of the stock and baste occasionally. Remove to a hot platter. Add the rest of the stock and ½ cup white wine to the sauce in the pan and cook until thickened. Remove the garlic clove. Pour sauce over chicken on the platter. Serves 6.

TWO

1 young chicken (3 to 3½ pounds)
5 tablespoons olive oil
salt and pepper to taste
parsley, few sprigs
1 bay leaf
1 small clove garlic
1 tablespoon flour
½ cup white wine
2 tablespoons tomato sauce
½ cup sliced mushrooms

Cut chicken into serving pieces. Brown on all sides in hot olive oil. Season with salt and pepper. Add a few sprigs parsley, bay leaf and garlic. Cover and simmer until almost tender, about 1½ hours. Remove chicken. Sprinkle flour over gravy and stir until smooth. Stirring constantly, gradually add wine, tomato sauce and mushrooms. Cook 10 minutes. Remove garlic. Serve chicken in hot sauce. Serves 6.

THREE

1 young chicken (3 to 3½ pounds)
3 tablespoons cooking fat
8 small white onions
8 small carrots
1½ cups red wine
½ clove garlic, minced
2 tablespoons flour
12 mushrooms
2 sprigs parsley
1 bay leaf
⅛ teaspoon dried thyme
salt and pepper to taste

Quarter chicken and brown in fat. Remove and brown onions and carrots lightly. Add ½ cup wine and remaining ingredients. Return chicken to pan. Cover tightly and simmer until chicken and vegetables are tender, about 1 hour. Add balance of wine as liquid cooks down. Serves 6.

POTATO PANCAKES

Sol and Dora Wilson give each year a breakfast party. The main dish is always their famous Polish Potato Pancakes:

1½ pounds potatoes
1 pint milk
3 eggs, separated
powdered cinnamon to taste
2 tablespoons butter
sugar to taste

Boil the potatoes. Rub them through a sieve into a bowl and mix with the milk, butter, the yolks of the eggs, cin-

namon, sugar and the egg whites beaten to a stiff foam. Beat into
a batter and cook as you would thin pancakes. Serve with sour
cream. Serves 6 to 8.

SPANISH RICE

Since the war has ended, Majorca seems to be the
terminal for most of the people who leave Cape Cod for the
winter, and they all are making Spanish Rice since their return.
And it's an appropriate dish for Cape Cod where clams and
mussels are to be had for the digging:

1 pint soft clams
1 pint mussels
1 cup rice
½ cup olive oil
2 onions, minced
1 clove garlic, minced
2 green peppers, minced
1 pimiento, chopped
3 cups crushed tomatoes
1 teaspoon saffron

Steam the clams and the mussels separately. Cook the rice in the oil until a golden brown. Add the onion, garlic, peppers and pimiento, and cook for about 5 minutes. Add the tomatoes and cook over a low flame until the rice is soft, adding clam juice slowly, and just enough to make the rice soft. Add the steamed clams and the mussels and more clam juice, if necessary. Stir in the saffron at the last. Serves 6 to 8.

I noticed in Mexico that the clams and the mussels are not included in this dish and that chili powder is used in place of the saffron. It was very delicious there, in the Mexican manner, too.

SPINACH SOUP

I'm sorry the Cacaces left Cape Cod before I found out how they seasoned spinach with anchovies. I'll always remember that dish. However, their spinch soup is as memorable:

2 pounds spinach
1 small onion, chopped fine
2 tablespoons butter
4 cups chicken stock
½ teaspoon salt
¼ teaspoon pepper
⅛ teaspoon nutmeg
1 egg
grated cheese

Cook the spinach in very little water. When it is tender, chop it very fine. Cook the onion in the butter. Add the spinach, stock and seasonings. Simmer for 10 minutes. Stir in the egg, well beaten. Cook until slightly thickened, without boiling. Serve with dry toast in each bowl and sprinkle lavishly with grated cheese. Serves 6 to 8.

BOUILLABAISSE

Bouillabaisse may be my favorite dish—or it only may be because it conjures up wonderful memories of Marseilles and the Cannebierre and long evenings on the terrace of little bistros in the *vieux port* there.

Lucille Donahue's Everbreeze is a small white informal restaurant a few doors from my house in Provincetown. Its terrace overhangs the harbor and, although Chateau d'If does not face it, some of the most beautiful sunsets in the world are reflected on the fishing fleet just offshore and on the distant Truro hills.

When Horace Titus heard that Lucille's chef was from Marseilles he took the place over one night for a party for his father's arrival in Provincetown. It was a large party, of course, and afterwards everybody on leaving sought the kitchen with nostalgic congratulations for making a dish they all loved in France so perfectly here on Cape Cod.

"But, Messieurs, it is not a perfect replica, I regret. In Marseilles it is imperative that I incorporate 26 different fish of many species in my bouillabaisse. But here many of them are not to be caught. There is no mullet, for instance."

fishing from the pier

But despite no mullet, Bouillabaisse Everbreeze is wonderful:

1 carrot
2 medium-sized onions, sliced
1 garlic clove, bruised
2 leeks, sliced
½ cup olive oil
3 pounds fish
2 large tomatoes
1 bay leaf
2 cups fish stock
1 dozen oysters, clams and mussels
½ cup lobster meat
½ cup canned pimiento, cut in small pieces
1 pinch saffron
salt and pepper to taste
juice of 1 lemon
1 tablespoon minced parsley
1 cup white wine

Cook carrot, onions, garlic and leeks in olive oil until golden brown. Add fish cut in 3-inch squares, tomatoes, bay leaf and stock. Simmer 20 minutes. Add shellfish, pimiento and saffron to taste. Season with salt, pepper and lemon juice.

Serve this wonderful dish in two courses: the liquid first in a deep soup plate over toast and sprinkled with parsley; the fish immediately after the soup plate has been removed. Flavor it slightly just before serving with a cup of heated white wine. Serves 6 to 8.

Lucille's chef finds it expedient here to limit himself to 3 or 4 different fish, whichever are in season—flounder, whiting, sole, haddock, perch, etc.

GOULASH

We go in the late afternoon to see Maurice Sterne's paintings in his studio. They are always heady and exciting and we don't need a cocktail, but we stay on and drink cocktails. And suddenly, without its being a "party," it is a party and there is Vera's famous Hungarian Goulash:

1 large onion, chopped
lard
paprika
salt to taste
1 pound pork
1 pound sauerkraut
½ cup sour cream

Brown the onion, chopped, in hot lard. Sprinkle with paprika and salt. Add the pork, cut into small squares, and a little water, and simmer until the water has evaporated. Keep repeating this process until the meat is tender. Add the sauerkraut, which should be previously boiled. Stir until it is all well mixed together. Add the sour cream, and blend over the fire. Serves 4.

Vera prefers to use goose fat in place of the lard, when she has goose fat.

Marjorie Mills' idea of goulash varies considerably from Vera's:

6 onions, sliced
melted fat
1½ pounds beef
1 clove garlic, crushed
1 tablespoon paprika
a few caraway seeds
salt and pepper to taste

Brown the onions, sliced, in melted fat in a casserole. Add the beef, cut in 1-inch cubes, the garlic, crushed, the paprika and the caraway seeds. Season with salt and pepper. Cover the casserole and cook until the meat is slightly browned. Add enough water, or a can of beef broth, to cover the meat and simmer for 1½ hours. Serve with noodles. Serves 4 to 6.

This third goulash recipe is one Mala Silson brought home from Mexico, as it is prepared there in the home of a Polish family by their Mexican cook; a fine example of an emigré losing its indentity in a foreign land:

¾ pound beef liver
½ cup chopped onions
⅓ cup chopped green peppers
3 tablespoons cooking oil
2 cups boiled tomatoes
⅓ cup chopped celery
1 clove garlic
2 teaspoons salt
⅛ teaspoon pepper
3 tablespoons flour
2 cups noodles, uncooked

Brown liver, cut into 1-inch cubes, together with the onions and the green peppers in the oil. Add the tomatoes, celery, garlic and seasoning. Simmer for ½ hour. Thicken with the flour mixed with a little water. Boil noodles separately in salt water. Drain. Serve the goulash over hot noodles. Serves 4.

The Colonial Inn

The Colonial Inn looks what a Colonial Inn should look like—a gracious building, rather three of them, in a setting of hollyhocks and elm trees and green lawns, and furnished with mellow mahogany, documentary wallpapers, flowered chintz and Georgian silver. The bar is paneled in oak, has mullioned windows which give onto the shipping in the harbor.

Naturally such a storybook setting is the scene of most of Provincetown's nicest parties; to meet Glenda Farrell and the cast from the theatre after the play on opening night; to hear

Julius Monk play; to say good-bye to Ione and Hudson Walker; to see a small fashion show from Paraphernalia; to meet Herbert Jacoby's friends; endlessly.

Mart Oliver guards a few of her recipes zealously, especially the now famous spiced marchel and a drink, that has no name as

yet, of vodka, gin and cucumber juice. I am sure all good cooks will feel appreciative to her, however, for allowing us to use the following, some of the most popular dishes in her inn:

SARDINE PUFFS HORS D'OEUVRE

PUFFS

¼ cup butter
½ cup bread flour
2 eggs, unbeaten

Add butter to ½ cup boiling water. Heat and beat until butter melts. When boiling, add flour all at once and stir vigorously until ball forms in center of pan. Remove from fire, let stand 5 minutes. Add 1 egg at a time, beating after each egg. Mixture should be very stiff. Drop mixture by spoonfuls onto greased tin sheets. Bake at 400° for 20 to 30 minutes. Makes about 40 puffs, hors d'oeuvre size.

FILLING

1 square cream cheese (8 ounces), mashed with 1 can sardines softened with sour cream.

FILLET OF SOLE WITH LOBSTER SAUCE

Poach fillets of sole or flounder in ½ water and ½ white wine. When cooked, pour off liquid. Place fish on serving platter and cover with lobster sauce.

LOBSTER SAUCE

3 tablespoons butter
3 tablespoons flour
1 cup liquid poured off fish
½ cup heavy cream
2 egg yolks
½ cup lobster meat, diced
salt
paprika
sherry to taste

Combine ingredients and stir over hot fire until creamy.

YORKSHIRE PUDDING

Cover the bottom of a bread pan with fat from roast beef. Heat the pan in oven while you combine:

2 eggs
1 cup flour
½ teaspoon salt
1 cup milk

in a mixing bowl and beat well. Pour into heated pans. Bake in hot oven 400°. When well puffed up, baste once or twice with beef fat from roast. Serve on platter with roast beef.

BEEF KIDNEY AND MUSHROOMS IN SOUR CREAM

1 pound beef kidney
2 tablespoons vinegar
1 large onion, chopped
1 pound mushrooms, sliced
1 cup sour cream
salt and pepper to taste

Skin and dice kidney. Soak in enough water to cover, with the vinegar. Bring to boil in this water and pour off. Cover with boiling water and add chopped onion. Cook until tender. Add sliced mushrooms. Just before serving, stir in sour cream. Season with salt and pepper. Serve with small potato pancakes. Serves 6.

POTATO PANCAKES

Grate 4 or 5 good-sized potatoes, drain off some of liquid. Add 2 eggs and Bisquick flour to form proper consistency. Fry in butter slowly. Make pancakes very thin.

FIG PUDDING

3 ounces beef suet
½ pound figs
2⅓ cups stale bread crumbs
½ cup milk
1 cup sugar
2 eggs, well-beaten
¾ teaspoon salt

Force beef suet and figs through food chopper and work together with hands until creamy. Soak stale bread crumbs in milk, add eggs, well beaten, sugar and salt. Combine mixtures. Fill buttered mold ¾ full. Steam 3 hours. Serves 6 to 8.

SAUCE

¼ cup butter
¾ cup confectioner's sugar
1 egg, separated
¾ cup heavy cream
rum or brandy to taste

Cream butter with sugar and egg yolk. Add egg white, beaten separately. Whip and add heavy cream. Flavor to taste with rum or brandy.

A SIMPLE, SEDUCTIVE
AND SUBTLE DESSERT

Pick from stems seedless white grapes. Wash and sprinkle with light brown sugar. Chill well. Serve with sour cream.

STRAWBERRY RUM
PARFAIT

Soak frozen sliced strawberries in several tablespoons of rum. Put strawberries in parfait glass. Then vanilla ice cream and whipped cream.

The Packet

"The Packet, High Brewster" is a delightful address and an antique collector's paradise. Bradford and Kay Clarke are famous hosts and it is now a famous fact that no one has ever turned down an invitiation to dine in their early pine house. The modern comforts and conveniences are all there but so carefully concealed and incorporated that people feel they are transported into the eighteenth century as soon as they've crossed the threshold; in less sure hands the whole place could seem entirely a stage setting. But the Clarkes have made an eighteenth-century house, furnished completely, even to the most minute detail, entirely livable in the twentieth century.

Kay loves to cook:

ONION ORMOLOO

10-12 large white onions
10-12 boiled white potatoes
1 cup milk
3 eggs
nutmeg
salt and pepper

Peel onions. Soak in cold water for about an hour, then boil until soft. Wash. Add an equal amount of boiled white potatoes. Add milk and eggs, well beaten. Beat mixture hard, season with nutmeg, salt and pepper. Bake in oven (350°) for 40-45 minutes. When half done, pour a little melted butter over top. Serves 6 to 8.

BISQUE TORTONI PIE

2 eggs, beaten
½ cup sugar
¾ teaspoon vanilla
salt to taste
1 cup milk
1 tablespoon gelatine
½ pint heavy cream
½ pound dried macaroons, crumbled

Make a soft custard with the eggs, sugar, vanilla, salt and milk. Remove from fire and allow to cool. Add the gelatine which has been softened for 5 minutes in 2 tablespoons of milk. When partially set, add the cream, whipped, and the macaroons. Place this mixture in a baked rich pie shell and place in refrigerator until wanted. Serves 4 to 6.

ESCALLOPED EGGPLANT

2 small onions
1 medium-sized eggplant, cubed
salt and pepper to taste
bread crumbs
butter

Saute chopped onions in butter, then add the eggplant, cubed, slightly brown, and salt and pepper. Put in baking dish, cover with the bread crumbs and dot with butter generously. Bake in medium oven (350°) for 35-40 minutes. Serves 4.

DATE BALLS

1 cup dates, cut fine
1 cup nuts
1 cup sugar
3 eggs, beaten separately
   (add beaten egg whites last)
⅔ cup flour
½ teaspoon vanilla
½ teaspoon salt
powdered sugar

Mix all these ingredients thoroughly and bake in medium oven (350°) in greased pan. Cut in 1-inch squares. While still warm, roll into balls and then roll in powdered sugar.

This may be used as a dessert by cutting in larger squares and putting either whipped cream or boiled custard over it.

I have enjoyed all these dishes as much I have enjoyed the house and the hours spent in the Clarke's antique shop and their "Country Store."

The Worthington Adventure
or, According to Her Children,

MOTHER'S MUSH

There is always bantering about this dish in the Worthington's house, but the whole family loves it, perhaps because, naturally, it never tastes exactly the same as it did the previous time.

It is perhaps the most pleasant way of clearing out whatever is left in the ice box.

Try out one or two onions in butter, blended with one egg, beaten, ½ can of mushroom soup and 1 large can of tomatoes.

Add any and all odds and ends of cooked meats that are leftovers in your ice box—steak, roast beef, chicken, pork, anything—and whatever vegetables are left over, too: carrots, beans, potatoes, corn, rice, peas, etc.

Season with salt, pepper and herbs to taste, cover with grated cheese and bread crumbs and bake in a moderate oven (350°) for 45 minutes.

SHISH KEBAB

Since the highway has been improved, widened and straightened, Truro has become a by-passed village, to the inhabitants' delight. It is an ancient place of ancient houses scattered over beautiful rolling moorland to the sea. Writers and painters have, for years, striven to keep their little village unspoiled. The new road now circles through the moors and people drive through Truro without realizing it.

But Truro contains one restaurant that is more than worth one's while exploring to find—and it really isn't too difficult to locate. The Blacksmith Shop retains only the name of the original use the building was erected for. It is a small place under a hill with an enclosed terrace that makes dining out-of-doors a delight.

The owner wisely keeps the menu to a half dozen exactingly prepared dishes. Shish Kebab is my favorite. While compiling this book I have endeavored to contact Lawrence and Murial Wright, but apparently they are away for the winter.

I have eaten this succulent dish so often at the Blacksmith Shop that my culinary senses assure me that this is their method of preparing it. If I am wrong, please forgive me for including a recipe that, although we have proven it's excellence, isn't quite worthy of yours:

Cut lamb into cubes about 2½ inches square, ½ inch thick. Marinate overnight in:

¼ cup olive oil
¼ cup lemon juice
2 tablespoons onion pulp
1 clove garlic, crushed
½ teaspoon salt
¼ teaspoon pepper
¼ teaspoon cloves
⅛ teaspoon mace

Arrange alternately on a spit: 1 piece of lamb, 1 slice of bacon, folded, 1 large mushroom cap, 1 piece of green pepper and 1 onion. Repeat the length of the spit and broil.

Boston and Marjorie Mills

There is no need for being in the doldrums in Boston. The panacea for that is to go to Marjorie Mills' broadcast.

Sometimes I think the discovery of new dishes is life to her—she goes everywhere, she dines everywhere and tells the world about it daily on Station WBZ.

Sometimes I think, and this I'm sure of, that it's her fabulous sense of friendship that is the predominant factor of her life. Everyone knows her, everyone dines with her and everyone appears on her program with her.

And she loves Cape Cod.

These four recipes are good examples from her collection and well show her sense of sophisticated experimenting in *haute cuisine:*

WATERCRESS SOUP

2 bunches watercress
1 quart chicken stock
½ pound lean pork, cubed
corn meal
2 tablespoons butter
1 small onion, chopped fine
salt and pepper
nutmeg
1 cup cream

Simmer the watercress, chopped fine, in the stock for 20 minutes. Cut the pork in small cubes and dip them in the corn meal. Cook over a low flame in the butter with the onion until both are a deep yellow color. Add the pork to the watercress, and cook for ½ hour with the seasonings. Add the cream last. Serves 6 to 8.

RICE OMELET

(SERVED WITH WILD GRAPE JELLY)

4 eggs
½ teaspoon salt
dash of pepper
4 tablespoons milk
⅓ cup boiled rice

Separate the egg whites from the yolks. Add salt and pepper to the whites and beat until stiff. Add milk to the yolks and beat until thick. Fold rice into the egg yolk mixture, then fold this into the beaten egg whites. Pour into a well-greased skillet and cook over a low flame until bottom and sides are a light brown. Place in oven and bake at 300° until the top of the omelet is done. Spread ½ with wild grape jelly or with currant jelly. Fold the other ½ over and serve immediately. Serves 2.

SALMON TIMBALES

3 tablespoons butter
2 tablespoons celery, chopped
1 tablespoon onion, chopped
1 tablespoon green pepper, chopped
⅓ cup soft bread crumbs
1 cup milk
1¼ cups flaked salmon, cooked
2 eggs, beaten
¾ teaspoon salt
⅛ teaspoon paprika
1 teaspoon lemon juice
½ teaspoon Worcestershire sauce

Melt butter, add celery, onion and green pepper and cook 1 or 2 minutes. Add bread crumbs, milk and fish and remove pan from fire. Stir in the eggs, salt, paprika, lemon juice and Worcestershire sauce. Pour into 4 greased shallow molds or custard cups, place in a pan of hot water and bake in a moderate oven (350°) about 30 minutes, or until the mixture is firm.

Unmold and serve with cream sauce and mushrooms. In this case we prefer canned mushrooms, heated in the cream sauce. Garnish with a dash of paprika and decorate with parsley. Serves 4.

Cream Sauce is easy to make:

4 tablespoons butter
4 tablespoons flour
1 cup milk
½ teaspoon salt
dash of pepper

Melt butter in saucepan. When it bubbles, add flour and mix until smooth. Add about ½ of the milk and stir over fire until smooth and boiling. Repeat until milk is used. Boil for 2 minutes.

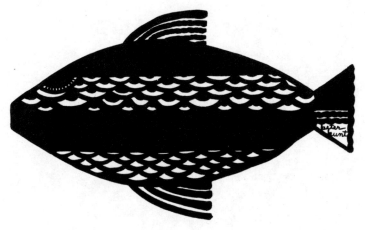

MEAT BALLS

I believe that this recipe stems from the Scandinavians. Being a peasant at heart I think it a very superior dish and wish that it could become universal in this country, replacing our inevitable hamburgers:

½ cup bread crumbs
2½ cups milk
2 eggs
½ pound minced beef
¼ pound minced veal
½ cup minced pork
2 tablespoons onions, chopped
salt and pepper
4 tablespoons butter

Soak the bread crumbs until they swell in the milk into which you have beaten the eggs. Work the meat into this. Add the onions, fried to a golden brown. Season with salt and pepper. Mold into small balls. Fry in butter until brown. Add 1 cup of boiling water and simmer for 15 minutes. Serves 4.

Sweets

"It seems rather silly to own lovely old things if you have no use for them. I can't understand women collecting fifty or a hundred pitchers when they only need two or three of them, or a lot of Sandwich glass to keep in cupboards. What I own I use, or I don't want it in the house." Helen Morton says this with a smile, of course—her house is an antique collector's paradise.

But it is also true that she does use all her antiques, and for what most of them were originally intended, which is unusual here; people grow philodendron in old bird cages, make door-stops of antique flatirons and lamps from milk cans.

We tease her that perhaps she learnt to make candy rather than not use the old candy jars she bought at auction last summer.

"Maybe. And why not? It's awfully easy to make" . . .

GLAZED NUTS

1 cup sugar
⅓ cup light corn syrup
1 pound assorted nuts, shelled

Combine sugar, syrup and ½ cup water in a small saucepan. Cook over low heat, stirring constantly until mixture boils. Continue cooking without stirring until candy thermometer registers 300° Wipe sugar crystals from sides of pan with a damp cloth during cooking period. Remove from heat. Drop several nuts at a time into syrup. Remove each one from the syrup separately with a fork. Place each one separately in a buttered pan. Keep them in a single layer until cooled.

CANDIED GRAPEFRUIT PEEL

2 large grapefruit
¼ cup light corn syrup
2 cups sugar

Wash grapefruit, remove peel in quarters; remove pulp and membrane. Cover peel with cold water and bring to boil. Cook 20 minutes. Drain off water; repeat cooking process. Boil until peel is tender. Drain, cool, and remove inner white membrane. Cut peel in ¼-inch strips. Combine corn syrup, sugar and 1 cup hot water. Cook over low heat, stirring until sugar is dissolved. Add grapefruit peel and cook until a little mixture forms very soft ball in cold water. Peel will be transparent and most of the syrup will be absorbed. Remove peel from syrup, drain. Roll each strip in granulated sugar.

CANDIED LEMON PEEL

Use above grapefruit recipe, but substitute peel from 6 lemons.

CANDIED ORANGE PEEL

Use above recipe, but substitute peel from 4 large oranges. Substitute 1 cup water in which orange peel was cooked for 1 cup hot water.

MOLASSES TAFFY

2 cups molasses
1 cup brown sugar
2 tablespoons butter
1 tablespoon vinegar
1 pinch baking soda

Boil together molasses, brown sugar, butter, ½ cup water, vinegar and baking soda. When a little of this syrup dropped in water becomes brittle, pour the taffy out on a buttered dish and let it cool. Rub some butter on the hands and pull the candy, small portions at a time, until it becomes a light honey color. Twist the thick strands into ropes and cut them into 1-inch pieces.

MAPLE NUT BRITTLE

1 cup light brown sugar
1 cup maple sugar
2 tablespoons butter
1 teaspoon vanilla
¼ teaspoon salt
1 cup walnut meats

Boil sugar in ½ cup water, until a little of the syrup dropped in water forms a firm ball. Add butter and boil to 300°. Add vanilla and salt. Pour the boiling syrup into a buttered pan over the walnuts. Break into pieces when cold.

Pecans are a nice alternate to walnuts.

FRENCH NOUGAT

1 cup strained honey
6 tablespoons light corn syrup
2 cups sugar
3 egg whites, beaten
1 cup blanched almonds, chopped
½ cup maraschino cherries, chopped
1 teaspoon almond extract

Boil honey, corn syrup, sugar and 1 cup water until a little dropped in water forms a hard ball. Beat egg whites until stiff. Slowly add the syrup, beating constantly. When the mixture begins to set, add blanched almonds and cherries, chopped coarsely, and almond extract. Pour mixture at once into buttered pans lined with wafer paper. Cover it with a sheet of wax paper, using a board and heavy weight to press the mixture flat. Cut into strips. Wrap each piece in wax paper.

PINEAPPLE MACEDOINE

Catherine Hazeltine lives in a beautiful Georgian house, restored with a perfection of taste. Her furniture is by Chippendale and Hepplewhite and Sheraton and all the appointments of her place are correct and of the period.

I have often surmised, and I hope correctly, although she laughs off my questioning her about it, that she has done research also for the foods of her period. It cannot be a coincidence, I feel, that the Lowestoft and the Waterford and the Chinese Porcelain plates should always have food apparently of the era of their origin.

In Irish glass boat-shaped bowls, resting on blue-edged and starred plates of Chinese origin, Catherine serves pineapples cut in half lengthwise. They are hollowed and the flesh, combined with halved green grapes, chopped dates, tangerines and

oranges cut small, is placed back in the shells. Heaped over the fruit is a frothing made from the white of eggs, beaten stiff with sugar and flavored with lemon juice, and all garnished slightly with chopped fresh mint leaves.

"In England I'd use fresh figs instead of these dried dates—why don't you have fresh figs on Cape Cod?" she mumbles querulously.

GINGER ICE

Another desert from Catherine Hazeltine . . .

I went into her kitchen and stayed there with her cook after dinner and cajoled her so as to find the source of this recipe. I have never had it anywhere else and I was curious to know where they had found it. Had they invented it or had they brought it back from another country?

"Lordy, we've always made it—for such a long time I have no idea which book we first read it in.

"I first make a pint of sugar syrup by cooking together, until medium thick, 1½ cups of sugar, 2 cups of water and a pinch of cream of tartar.

"While it is cooling, I chop ¼ pound of preserved ginger into a paste, adding 1 or 2 tablespoons of the syrup.

"Then I grate the rind of 1 orange and add it and the juice of the same orange, and the juice of 2 lemons to the ginger paste and blend well before I pour the sugar syrup into it, beating and stirring until everything is well blended.

"Cool and freeze just long enough for it all to become a mush.

"Then beat in the white of 1 egg, stiffly beaten, and freeze firmly." Serves 6.

Fruit Cake and Variations

What a difference in opinion! What a discussion at Orin and Midge Tourov's party.

Maybe fifty people were there to meet Virginia Payne who is "Ma Perkins" in Orin's famous radio play. Fruit cake was with the dessert and when everyone exclaimed that it was the finest fruit cake they had ever eaten I, of course, went into the kitchen to get the recipe from Courtney.

"I worked on it for eight hours and watched it for four." I stayed in the kitchen so long that people came in to see why I wasn't back in the party and by degrees the rest of the evening became a discussion on preparing fruit cake. I collected a nice batch of favorite methods for preparing this festive cake —and several amazing derivations of it:

FRUITCAKE

1 cup candied pineapple, cut in 1-inch pieces
1 cup candied cherries
½ cup candied orange peel, finely cut
½ cup candied lemon peel, finely cut
3 tablespoons citron, finely cut
⅓ cup shortening
3 tablespoons brown sugar
3 tablespoons honey
2 eggs, well beaten
½ cup flour
½ teaspoon salt
½ teaspoon baking powder
dash allspice
dash nutmeg
2 tablespoons orange juice
3½ cups pecan halves

Wash the sugar from the candied fruits and dry on paper toweling. Cream shortening and brown sugar. Add honey and beat. Add eggs and beat. Sift together flour, salt, baking powder, and spices; add, alternately with orange juice, to the creamed mixture. Line cake pan with 2 thicknesses of waxed paper; grease top layer. Spread ⅓ of batter over bottom. Save some cherries and nuts for the top. Add rest of fruits and nuts to remaining batter in pan; pack it down and smooth top with spoon. Decorate with cherries and nuts. Cover with brown paper. Set in pan of water, for the first hour of baking, and bake in slow oven (300°) about 2 hours. When cool, glaze with hot corn syrup. Cut in 2-inch squares.

DARK FRUITCAKE

1 cup dried apricots, sliced
1½ cups prunes, cut up
2 cups seedless raisins
1½ cups seeded raisins
1½ cups currants
1½ cups dates, sliced
2½ cups preserved citron, diced
1½ cups preserved pineapple, diced
1½ cups candied cherries, halved
1 cup preserved orange peel, diced
1 cup preserved lemon peel, diced
1½ cups blanched almonds, slivered
1 cup pecan halves, chopped
3 cups flour, sifted
2 teaspoons allspice
2 teaspoons cinnamon
1½ teaspoons nutmeg
1 teaspoon mace
½ teaspoon ginger
½ teaspoon powdered cloves
½ teaspoon baking soda
1½ teaspoons salt
1 cup shortening
1½ cups brown sugar
6 eggs, unbeaten
½ cup molasses
⅔ cup strawberry jam

Line 2 tube pans with 2 thicknesses greased brown paper and 1 thickness greased waxed paper.

Rinse apricots, prunes; cover with water; boil 5 minutes. Drain; cool. Cut prunes from pits into pieces; slice apricots. Rinse and drain raisins, currants; then add to prunes and apricots. Add dates, citron, pineapple, cherries, orange peel and lemon peel. Sliver almonds; chop pecans coarsely; add both to fruits. Sprinkle 1 cup flour over all; mix well. Sift remaining 2 cups flour with allspice, cinnamon, nutmeg, mace, ginger, powdered cloves, baking soda and salt. Thoroughly beat shortening with brown sugar until very light and fluffy, then with eggs, one at a time, until very creamy. Slowly beat in alternately, in fourths, flour mixture, molasses, and jam just until smooth. Pour over fruit-nut mixture; mix well. Pack lightly into pans. Bake, with small shallow pan of hot water on floor of oven (300°), until done, 3 to 3½ hours. Cool completely in pan on wire rack. Remove from pan; peel off paper.

FRUITCAKE
WITH BRAZIL NUTS

3 cups Brazil nuts, shelled
2 packages dates, pitted
1 cup maraschino cherries, drained
¾ cup flour, sifted
¾ cup granulated sugar
½ teaspoon baking powder
½ teaspoon salt
3 eggs, beaten
1 teaspoon vanilla

Grease loaf pan and line with waxed paper.

Place nuts, dates and cherries in a large bowl. Sift together flour, sugar, baking powder and salt over nut and fruit mixture; mix with hands until nuts and fruits are well coated. Beat eggs until foamy; add vanilla; stir into nut mixture until well mixed. Spread in pan evenly. Bake in 300° oven for 2 hours. Cool in pan on wire rack 15 minutes. Remove from pan; peel off paper; cool on rack. Wrap in aluminum foil; then store in refrigerator.

FRUITCAKE
WITH WALNUTS

2 cups walnuts, broken up
2 teaspoons butter
2 cups seedless raisins
1 cup golden raisins
1 cup pitted dates, chopped
1 pound mixed preserved fruits, diced
2½ cups flour, sifted
1 cup granulated sugar
1½ teaspoons baking powder
1 teaspoon salt
1 cup shortening
½ cup honey
⅓ cup orange juice
1 tablespoon lemon juice
4 eggs, unbeaten

Spread broken walnuts in shallow pan; dot with butter. Rinse raisins in cold water; place in covered casserole. Bake both 15 to 20 minutes, or until nuts are toasted (350°). Remove from oven.

Grease 2 loaf pans; line with 2 layers wrapping paper and 1 layer waxed paper, greasing layers generously.

Combine toasted nuts, raisins, dates and preserved fruits in a bowl; sift 1 cup flour over these; mix well. Sift 1½ cups flour with sugar, baking powder, salt, into a large mixing bowl. Drop in shortening; pour in honey, fruit juices. Beat 2 minutes. Add eggs, one at a time, beating thoroughly after each addition; beat 1 minute more. Pour batter over floured nut-fruit mixture; stir until well mixed. Spoon into pans. Bake in 300° oven, with small shallow pan of water on floor of oven, until no imprint remains when cake top is touched by finger tips. Cool completely in pans on wire rack. Remove from pans; peel off papers.

DE LUXE FRUIT CAKE

1 cup shortening
1½ cups brown sugar
4 eggs
3 cups flour, sifted
1 teaspoon baking powder
2 teaspoons salt
2 teaspoons cinnamon
2 teaspoons allspice
1 teaspoon cloves
1 cup orange juice, boiling hot
1 cup citron, thinly sliced
1 cup candied pineapple, chopped
1½ cups candied cherries, whole
1 cup raisins
1 cup figs, chopped
3 cups nuts, coarsely chopped

Mix together shortening, brown sugar and eggs. Beat vigorously with spoon for 2 minutes. Sift together 2 cups of the flour, baking powder, salt, cinnamon, allspice and cloves. Stir into shortening mixture alternately with boiling hot orange juice. Mix remaining cup of flour into citron, pineapple, cherries, raisins, figs and nuts. Pour batter over fruit, mixing thoroughly. Line 2 greased loaf pans with brown paper. Pour batter into the pans. Place a pan of water on lower oven rack. Bake cakes 3 hours in slow oven (275°). After baking, let cakes stand 15 minutes before removing from pans. Cool thoroughly on racks without removing paper. When cool, remove paper. Store by wrapping tightly in aluminum foil, then put in covered jar in a cool place to ripen.

CHRISTMAS PUDDING

½ pound beef suet, chopped
¼ pound currants
½ pound sultana raisins
½ pound raisins, stoned
¼ pound mixed peel, shredded
peel of 1 lemon, chopped
½ of a grated nutmeg
½ ounce mixed spice
½ ounce ground cinnamon
½ pound bread crumbs
2 ounces almonds, shredded
2 ounces flour
pinch salt
1 cup milk
4 eggs
4 ounces rum
juice of 1 lemon, strained

Skin the suet and chop it fine. Clean the fruit, stone the raisins, finely shred the mixed peel; peel and chop the lemon rind. Put all the dry ingredients in a bowl and mix well. Add the milk, stir in the eggs one at a time, add the rum and the strained juice of the lemon. Mix all thoroughly. Put the mixture in a well-greased mold. Steam for 5 hours.

STEAMED FRUIT PUDDING

1 cup flour
1 teaspoon baking soda
1 teaspoon salt
1 teaspoon cinnamon
¼ teaspoon nutmeg
¼ teaspoon cloves
3 cups soft bread crumbs
1 cup cream
½ cup melted shortening
½ cup molasses
1 cup seedless raisins
¾ cup mixed fruits and peels

Sift together flour, soda, salt, cinnamon, nutmeg and cloves. Pour cream over bread crumbs in a bowl. Add shortening and molasses; stir until well blended; add flour mixture. Then stir in raisins, mixed fruits and peels; mix well. Pour into well-greased mold. Pour water to depth of 1 inch into deep kettle with rack; place mold on rack. Cover kettle tightly; bring to boil; reduce heat and steam 3 hours. Uncover kettle; let stand for 5 minutes, then remove pudding and unmold. Serve warm with maraschino sauce.

MARASCHINO SAUCE

Cream 4 tablespoons butter in a bowl, add 1½ cups sifted confectioner's sugar; mix well. Stir in 1 tablespoon maraschino cherry syrup, beat with wooden spoon until smooth and fluffy; stir in 2 tablespoons finely chopped marschino cherries.

FRUITCAKE CONFECTION

½ cup sifted flour
½ teaspoon salt
½ teaspoon baking powder
⅛ teaspoon allspice
⅛ teaspoon nutmeg
⅓ cup shortening
3 tablespoons brown sugar
3 tablespoons honey
2 eggs, unbeaten
2 tablespoons orange juice
1 cup preserved pineapple, diced
½ cup preserved orange peel, diced
½ cup preserved lemon peel, diced
¼ cup preserved citron, diced
1 cup candied cherries
3½ cups pecan halves

Line layer-cake pan with 2 thicknesses waxed paper, then grease.

Sift together flour, salt, baking powder, allspice and nutmeg. Thoroughly mix shortening with sugar, then with honey and eggs, until very light and fluffy. Then slowly beat in, alternately, flour mixture and orange juice, just until smooth. Spread one third of batter over bottom of cake pan. To rest of batter, add fruits and pecans (reserving a few cherries and pecans for top); pile mixture on top of batter in pan, packing down and leveling top. Decorate with reserved cherries and nuts. Cover with brown paper; tie securely. Set in shallow pan of hot water. Bake in 350° oven for 1 hour. Remove from water; bake 1 hour longer. When done, brush top with hot corn syrup. Cool completely in pan on wire rack. Remove from pan; peel off paper.

FRUIT PIE

½ cup flour
1 cup sugar
1 cup suet
3 eggs
¾ cup brown sugar
2 tablespoons butter
2 cups finely cut citron
¾ cup seeded raisins
3 tablespoons vinegar
grated rind of ½ lemon
grated rind of ½ orange
½ teaspoon cinnamon
½ teaspoon grated nutmeg
½ cup cooking brandy
1 tablespoon cornstarch

Cook the above ingredients (excepting cornstarch) with 2 cups of water in a saucepan for 12 minutes.

Thicken with 1 tablespoon cornstarch mixed with cold water. When cool, pour into pie plate lined with pastry. Cover the top decoratively with pastry strips. Bake in hot oven until brown.

FRUIT ROLLS

2 tablespoons butter
2 tablespoons sugar
2 cups flour
4 teaspoons baking powder
½ teaspoon cinnamon
½ teaspoon salt
⅔ cup milk
½ cup currants
½ cup chopped dates

Blend butter and sugar. Sift together flour, baking powder, cinnamon and salt. Add to sugar mixture alternately with the milk. Mix currants and dates in a little of the flour and add last. Bake in moderate oven (350°).

Drinks

FISH HOUSE PUNCH

Who doesn't know the Flagship doesn't know Cape Cod. Everybody comes here for a lobster or a steak broiled over charcoal, or for Pat's famous ham steak broiled with sliced pineapple—everybody is happy here: Lily Pons and André Kostelanetz, Nancy Hamilton, Henrietta Holland, Helena Rubinstein, and one autumn night Mrs. Roosevelt came in out of the rain and wrote about the architecture and the decorations in her column shortly afterwards.

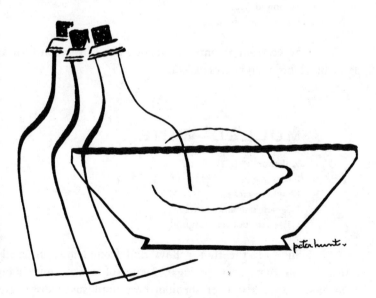

Pat has indeed built a unique restaurant on its own private wharf from driftwood and dunnage he collected on our back shore. Ship models are everywhere. His bar has been copied often all over the country. It is a halved dory. Lobster buoys and things from wrecks hang from the rafters. The accumulation of candle drippings in the bottles on each table has reached fantastic height and design through the years, rivaling those in the *Lapin Agile* which had at least fifty years' start, I should imagine, on Pat's. It's a wonderful place full of violin music in the summer and just as wonderful in the autumn—with tables pulled up before the cavernous fireplace.

The opening of the Flagship each spring is a great gala. Fish House Punch is the traditional drink that day.

Dilute every 2 quarts of water with

1 quart Jamaica Rum
1 quart Bacardi
1 quart Cognac
¾ pound sugar
1 quart lemon juice

Serve from an antique wooden bowl in which float a large block of ice and slices of lemon.

MULLED WINE

½ lemon
1 cup sugar
18 whole cloves
2 3-inch cinnamon sticks
2 ⅘-quart bottles Burgundy

Slice off the thin yellow rind from lemon in small strips. Put in saucepan with sugar, 3 cups of water, cloves and cinnamon sticks. Stir over medium heat until sugar dissolves.

Boil gently for 10 minutes. Strain into double boiler; add Burgundy, heat over hot water. Serve hot with a cinnamon stick in each glass. This is a proverbial between-Christmas-and-New Year afternoon party drink in many Cape Cod homes. It is more festive and less heady than cocktails, of course—but heady.

EGGNOG

12 eggs, separated
1 pound sugar
1 bottle brandy or bourbon
1½ cups rum, Puerto Rican
½ cup rum, Jamaica
2½ quarts milk
1 pint cream
powdered nutmeg

Beat egg whites. Beat yolks, add to them sugar, brandy, rum, and mix. Add milk, cream and mix. When well blended, turn into punch bowl. Turn the stiffly-beaten egg whites on top. Dust with nutmeg. Then call your neighbors in and have a Merry Christmas.

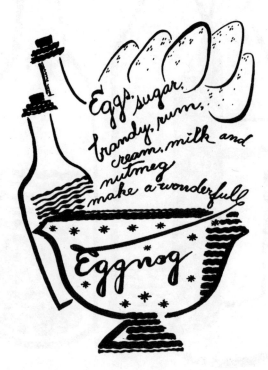

Eggs, sugar, brandy, rum, cream, milk and nutmeg make a wonderful Eggnog

Index

Our Own Recipes

APPETIZERS

Our Own Recipes

AND SOUPS

Our Own Recipes

FISH AND

Our Own Recipes

SEAFOOD

Our Own Recipes

MEAT AND

Our Own Recipes

POULTRY

Our Own Recipes

VEGETABLES

Our Own Recipes

AND SALADS

Our Own Recipes

DESSERTS

Our Own Recipes

AND DRINKS

The Author and his Book

PETER HUNT was born in New York City and grew up in a New Jersey suburb. He has become so identified with Cape Cod—and particularly with Provincetown—that most people think of him as a native Cape Codder. But he had never visited the Cape until, some thirty-five years ago, cruising to Maine, a storm forced the yacht on which he was a passenger to take shelter in Provincetown harbor. After that trip, he went back to Provincetown to see why he had liked it so much on that first short visit. He has been part of that community ever since. A gifted painter, he was one of the leaders in the rediscovery of folk art and, as the years have passed, he has concentrated increasingly on the application of folk art motifs to making everyday living more colorful and enjoyable. His Peasant Village group of shops at Provincetown draws thousands of visitors each year and a new shop at Orleans is also prospering.